The Hiking Handbook for Beginners

The 10-Step Guide to Hiking

Samantha and Johnny Evans

© Copyright 2022 - All rights reserved.

The content contained within this book may not be reproduced, duplicated or transmitted without direct written permission from the author or the publisher.

Under no circumstances will any blame or legal responsibility be held against the publisher, or author, for any damages, reparation, or monetary loss due to the information contained within this book, either directly or indirectly.

Legal Notice:

This book is copyright protected. It is only for personal use. You cannot amend, distribute, sell, use, quote or paraphrase any part, or the content within this book, without the consent of the author or publisher.

Disclaimer Notice:

Please note the information contained within this document is for educational and entertainment purposes only. All effort has been executed to present accurate, up to date, reliable, complete information. No warranties of any kind are declared or implied. Readers acknowledge that the author is not engaged in the rendering of legal, financial, medical or professional advice. The content within this book has been derived from various sources. Please consult a licensed professional before attempting any techniques outlined in this book.

By reading this document, the reader agrees that under no circumstances is the author responsible for any losses, direct or indirect, that are incurred as a result of the use of the information contained within this document, including, but not limited to, errors, omissions, or inaccuracies.

Table of Contents

INTRODUCTION 1

CHAPTER 1: HEALTH - FITNESS AND PREVENTING INJURY IS KEY 4

    MENTAL AND PHYSICAL BENEFITS OF EXERCISE 4
    GETTING IN SHAPE FOR HIKING 7
    INJURY PREVENTION 9
    HIKING TECHNIQUES 12

CHAPTER 2: CHOOSING THE RIGHT GEAR 15

    CLOTHING 15
    BAGS 19
    STICKS/WALKING POLES 21
    RAIN GEAR 23
    FIRST AID 25
    OTHER USEFUL ITEMS 27
    WOMEN AND CHILDREN SPECIFIC GEAR 28

CHAPTER 3: CHOOSING A ROUTE 31

    THE HIKE 31
    KEEPING SAFE AS A SOLO WALKER 35
    PERMITS 37

CHAPTER 4: WHAT TO DO IN THE EVENT OF AN EMERGENCY 40

    ASSESS THE SITUATION 40
    NON-EMERGENCY 42
    MEDICAL EMERGENCY 47
    WHAT TO DO IF YOU GET LOST 49

CHAPTER 5: WEATHER - ENSURING THE CONDITIONS DO NOT RUIN THE HIKE 51

    KNOW YOUR LIMITS 51
    INFLUENCE OF THE SEASONS 53
    MAKE A PLAN AND ADAPT 54

CHAPTER 6: FOOD AND WATER 59

    NUTRITION 59
    HYDRATION 62

CHAPTER 7: NAVIGATION 64
  GETTING AROUND...64
  ARE YOU ALLOWED TO BE HERE? 68

CHAPTER 8: ETIQUETTE 69
  THE COUNTRYSIDE CODE 69
  BATHROOM BREAKS 72
  POTENTIAL PENALTIES 73
  PERSONAL AND ENVIRONMENTAL HEALTH 74

CHAPTER 9: HIKING WITH CHILDREN AND PETS 76
  CHILDREN 76
  PETS 78

CHAPTER 10: OVERNIGHT HIKING 80
  KEY CONSIDERATIONS 80

CONCLUSION 85

BONUSES 87

REFERENCES 93

Introduction

Hiking is a remarkable activity for the simple fact that it walks the line between being a strenuous sporting venture and a pleasant day out in nature. It is an excellent way to stay or become fit and healthy while providing a beautiful opportunity to engage with the wonders of the natural world. Hiking is the natural next step for anyone who enjoys the outdoors and going for walks. It is, however, very daunting to start, and seems to require so much information that is not readily accessible to beginners. So much of the information available is targeted at veteran hikers looking to push their limits. We are Samantha and Johnny and we absolutely love hiking. Our goal with this book is to bridge that gap. We hope to share with you the fundamentals of what you need in order to be able to hike and gradually take on more challenging distances and inclines, working your way up to hikes lasting from dawn till dusk. For us, it has been a long journey of trial and error but we are now in a place to share that hard-won information and make this a more accessible hobby for everyone to enjoy. Hiking does not have to be intimidating, and people of all ages and abilities can and should enjoy it. We are here to tell you how.

It seems fitting to start out by telling you that neither of us are athletes. We are not naturally physical. We suffer from some underlying health conditions and have not always been particularly active. We have not grown up hiking and taking on these types of challenges. We do, however, share an undying love for this world. There is nothing that can compare to the joy of being outside in the sunshine, trekking along and taking in the sheer beauty around us. We have always loved to walk and spend time outdoors. We have a wonderful dog who now accompanies us on many of our hikes, and we have always strived to be active. Our first serious hike was an unqualified disaster. We were not prepared in terms of gear, physicality, and technique. The weather turned nasty on us and we ached for days afterward. We managed to reach the peak but the pain we endured almost eclipsed our achievement. This could have been the end of our hiking journey but we decided to persevere—and this was one of the best choices we have ever made. We want this guidebook to allow others to avoid the pitfalls that tripped us up along the way. We want to tell you that you can do this and offer you some helpful tips on how.

We discovered long ago that the gym is not the place for us. We do not want to spend our time sweating in a musty and overcrowded space, battling to find a gap to use the machines. We want to be healthy and fit but we want to achieve this with the wind in our hair and the sun on our faces. If you have ever felt like you cannot get healthy because of an aversion to the gym, if you have ever felt that you want to push yourself but do not know how to do so safely, and if you love the outdoors and want this to be central in your fitness journey, then this book will help you. We know what it is like to be daunted by taking the first step, and through our own journey, we discovered that there is so much variety and versatility in hiking that anyone can do it. You are not too old, out of shape, or inflexible to start. We have written this guide as a way of sharing what we have learned. Whether you are an absolute beginner or a seasoned short distance hiker looking to expand your range, you will benefit from this book.

In the following pages, you will learn the fundamentals of hiking from training and technical advice, to the gear you do and do not need. We will take you through the process of adequately planning a hike across differing levels of ability and regardless of impediments. You will learn about emergency situations, and not only how to deal with them, but about taking steps to avoid them. You will learn about hydration and nutrition and how to fuel your body to take on longer and more challenging trails. You will learn about the seasons and how rain or snow need not put you off a day in the wild. You will learn about hiking in different environments and in different contexts. If you are looking to hike with your children or with a dog, we've got some tips for you too. We will teach you how to navigate with confidence and find your way, no matter the challenges. Irrespective of your background or level of ability, hiking will be for you. We've even included some tips on how to move into overnight hiking and some bonuses like a customizable workout plan, a first aid cheat sheet, and a checklist for your first big day out. This book is a step-by-step guide that will show you how to take on this hobby safely and sustainably.

Standing at the bottom of a trail and looking up at it winding its way through wilderness to a seemingly distant peak can be so overwhelming. Hiking is as much a mental test as a physical one, but with preparation, you will be able to beat this anxiety. Whether you need some advice on conditioning or mental fortitude, we are here to help. It is always so much easier to give up than to put in the work, but we truly hope that the knowledge we share in this book will help you to gain the confidence it takes to hit the mountains, forests, or valleys with enthusiasm. The benefits of hiking go far beyond the physical. Hiking is a way for us to clear our minds and tackle the challenges we meet. It will grow your confidence and show you what you are truly capable of. Whether you aim at faraway peaks or deep forests, the sense of freedom you get from hiking is truly unmatched. The beginning of this journey may not be easy, but we promise you that it will be worthwhile.

Chapter 1:

Health - Fitness and Preventing Injury Is Key

Your body can make or break a hike, and so you need to treat it with respect. We started hiking from a position of not being particularly fit and you should know that this is absolutely possible. We worked on it, and grew and developed to a point where we felt confident taking on new challenges, higher peaks, and greater distances. As with any exercise, the more you do it, the easier it will become. In this first chapter, we will look at some ways of ensuring that you are physically able to complete any hike you set your mind to. Taking some steps to ensure that you are fit enough to complete longer hikes is not only beneficial to your health but also your mental stamina and confidence. The stronger you get, the easier the trails will become and you will be ready to try new and more challenging paths. A great rule of thumb with all aspects of hiking is to know that there is no such thing as being overprepared. The more you do, the more you will benefit. This is true of anything, but particularly hiking. You can enjoy this hobby at any level of fitness but the fitter you get, the more trails will open up to you, and the more you can explore.

Mental and Physical Benefits of Exercise

Everyone knows that exercise is great for your health. The more active you are, the better you will feel, and the less likely you are to develop chronic conditions. The key is to know your body and listen to it. Push yourself in safe and sustainable ways and the benefits will be plentiful. The CDC (Centers for Disease Control and Prevention) has published statistics that show how physical activity will improve brain health and development, improve bone strength, help with managing weight, and reduce the risk of disease. This requires simply that you do moderate exercise. A simple daily stroll in the park will help you in this regard. Moderate exercises like this are also a great way to begin conditioning yourself for hiking. It is important, however, to set goals and targets and ensure that you are on an upward trajectory. Try to increase your distance and pace as you go.

The pressures of daily life often mean that we cannot simply hike to our hearts' content, and so it is important that we supplement our exercise routines with activity as frequently as possible. Walking, running, yoga, squats, mountain climbing, and jumping rope are all great cardio exercises that you can do at home. These will keep you at an even level of fitness and prevent physical stagnation. The CDC recommends 150 minutes a week of exercise. This simply means 30 minutes of exercise a day, five times a week. This may seem a simple enough goal, but it is important that you are able to commit to this routine. We recommend trialing new exercises too. If you are not enjoying certain exercises, you will find it increasingly difficult to commit to doing them. So, try out new things constantly and incorporate those you like into your routine. Simply doing the same workout every single day is going to get boring and you may find that your physical progress plateaus. Variety makes your workouts more dynamic and you will find that your progress becomes easier and more fulfilling.

Exercising regularly will help you prevent so many common afflictions in later life. Moderate exercise will help you to avoid heart disease and strokes. Working out will keep your heart healthy and ensure healthy blood pressure and cholesterol levels. You will also lower your risk of developing type two diabetes and certain cancers such as lung and bladder. On top of that, it will allow you to manage your weight effectively and keep it off. These are all benefits of moderate exercise and are quite general. Let's get back to hiking.

Hiking is a full body exercise and conditions you from head to toe. On a day hike, you will be using all major muscle groups in your body. It is such a dynamic activity, as you are forced to move in different ways and constantly adapt to the environment. This, in conjunction with varying levels of strain due to elevations and dips, is incredibly beneficial to cardiovascular health. It is also an effective way of burning calories and developing muscle tone throughout the body. Hiking has also been shown to be incredibly beneficial to bone strength and density, while also naturally allowing you to keep your joints agile without the excess strain of higher impact sports. This is a great way to prevent conditions such as brittle bones, osteoporosis, and arthritis in later life.

Hiking also contributes majorly to lower body strength. We live in an age where exercise has been intertwined with aesthetics, and so there has been an increased emphasis on upper body strength. Our lower bodies are, however, the basis of most of our movements throughout our life (very few people walk around on their hands). Hiking will strengthen all the major muscles in the lower body from your quads, to hamstrings, to glutes. This will have a great impact on your balance, reflexes, and perhaps most importantly, your posture and spinal health. All of these benefits are going to allow you to move through life with increasing ease and grace. Hiking is also a venture with a great degree of variety and scalability. Whatever your level of fitness or expertise, there is certainly a hike for you. The benefits certainly do not end here.

Mental health is becoming an increasingly important element of our lives. There is an intrinsic link between physical and mental health in that exercise, generally, releases dopamine and allows us to break negative thought patterns. By working out, we can address anxiety and depression by devoting our focus to what is immediately in front of us. Hiking does all this and more. Firstly, you will generally need to be outdoors if you hope to hike. Simply being out in the sunshine has numerous health benefits derived from the fact that our bodies are absorbing vitamin D. Vitamin D is great for bone strength, too, and contributes to stronger teeth and muscles. Too much sunshine can be negative, so don't forget the sunscreen! Being outside also allows us to gain a sense of calm simply from breathing fresh air and experiencing the beauty in the sights and sounds around us.

Leaving the house and entering a new domain among the trees has an inherently calming effect. This allows us to naturally deal with stress, anxiety, and reduce the risk of depression. There is simply nothing like a day out on the trails to take you away from your day-to-day worries.

We are products of nature, and so the gentler sounds and softer sights will innately bring out a sense of well-being that is easily lost in the hustle and bustle of the city. Lastly, hiking can be a great social activity. Whether you hike with your dog or in a big group, you are achieving an aim with other individuals, and this, too, is a major way of dealing with anxiety or stress. Even if you prefer to hike alone, the brief interactions with others on the trail can leave you with a sense of social engagement.

Getting in Shape for Hiking

While hiking will work toward improving your fitness, it is important that you have a physical baseline from which to work. Many brave souls have ventured out on the trail thinking it will be an easy walk, only to be battered by the level of fitness required. It is important that you know your level of physicality first before testing yourself on a strenuous hike. Test yourself in safer environments close to home. Go for strolls around your neighborhood where you can walk fast enough to increase your heart rate. Try to do this at least three times a week and for at least 30 minutes at a time. This can form part of your training routine, but more importantly, it will show you what you are capable of. This is a great way to gauge your level of fitness before putting it to the test on a trail. It is important that you are honest with yourself in this process. If you struggle on the walks, there is absolutely no shame in that; it simply means you need a few more weeks before the hike. On the other hand, if you are walking at a good pace and for reasonable distances without feeling particularly tired, then you can rest assured that you are ready for some entry-level hikes.

Something else to consider is a visit to your doctor. General check-ups are always a good idea, and this can also help you to establish any underlying conditions. You do not want to find out about a medical condition in the middle of a hike. A dawn to dusk hike can be seriously strenuous at stages, and you need to know that you are healthy enough to attempt something like that before embarking. Remember that this should be something you are doing for yourself. It's not a race or a competition, and so you should never put your health at risk to rush progress. Take the time it takes and give yourself enough time to be truly ready. Building up stamina slowly before attempting your first hike will put you in a far better position to complete it with confidence. If you try to rush the process, you will run the risk of injuring yourself, or even ruining the experience and discouraging yourself from trying again.

Let's move on to some specific exercises you should incorporate into your routine to ensure you are ready for a day on the trails. Firstly, you could try walking or running in the sand. This is a really effective way of building strength in both your knees and ankles. This can be incredibly helpful for hiking, as these joints often take the brunt of the strain as you trek. If you do not have access to sand, you might also try lunges, reverse lunges, squats, and knee lifts to strengthen these important muscles. The stronger your knees and ankles are, the less likely you will be to injure yourself. A diverse range of motion is also very important for hiking fitness, and so you could stretch with a resistance band in order to strengthen muscles throughout a full extension. Trying to stand on a balance board of some kind or even simply a tennis ball will also be effective in terms of increasing the range of motion in your ankles.

Core strength is also vital for any keen hikers. Crunches, forearm planks, and leg lifts are really effective core workouts. A strong core will ensure better balance, which is important for uneven surfaces. Upper body strength is also very important, especially on hikes where you will carry a heavy pack. Simple at-home exercises such as push-ups, floor dips, inchworms, and shoulder presses are a great way to increase strength. If possible, free weight workouts such as bicep curls, dumbbell rows, and overhead presses will also work to strengthen your upper body. Lastly, any kind of cardio workout will help you with your general fitness level and will be vastly beneficial for hiking. Running, walking, and riding a stationary bike are great examples of cardio workouts that will improve the conditioning in your legs and general fitness. Please consult an expert if you are at all unsure about any of the above suggestions.

Injury Prevention

When training for your first hike, it is very important to consider ways in which you may get injured and work toward avoiding them. A sprained ankle or strained knee may keep you off the trails for an extended period and may even discourage you from picking up the hobby again once recovered. Let's look at some ways to ensure this does not happen. Firstly, it is vital that you prepare yourself for your specific gear. Blisters are a common minor trail injury that can be avoided fairly simply. When you train, try to wear your trail shoes or boots in order to get used to them. Wearing shoes for the first time on a hike is a surefire way to develop some nasty blisters. It is also best that you wear socks that fit snugly and do not shift as you walk. Make sure that you are prepared for varying levels of difficulty and note that we always recommend some kind of ankle support in your footwear to doubly protect you against strains and sprains. You should also prepare yourself to carry a pack for the duration of a hike. Work up to this gradually by training with it on your back and incrementally increasing the weight within until you have reached the actual weight it will be on the trail.

Sprains are also very common hiking injuries and can be a little more complex to avoid. Range of motion exercises are an excellent way to strengthen our joints and allow them to handle uneven surfaces better; however we need to supplement this with vigorous stretching in order to prepare ourselves as best we can. It is important to stretch thoroughly before and after any hike. Do not stretch at home; rather, aim to do it at the base of the trail on either end of the hike. We were once on a hike and one of us slipped and fell down a steeper section of trail, spraining an ankle in the process. Recovery was a drawn out process, but because of that injury, we were able to learn about the importance of stretching. Since then, we both stretch vigorously at all stages of a hike, and our ankles and joints are far more resilient than they were at the time of that injury. Let's break down some effective stretches that you should try.

Before the hike begins, you could start by stretching out your calves and quads. As your legs take much of the strain on a hike, it is vital that you adequately prepare these muscles. For calves, you could find a tree to lean against with the palms of your hands, while your arms are at a full stretch. Keep your toes pointed toward the tree and alternate legs as you bend them at the knee. This should look like a high lunge with your front knee bent to a little more than 90°. Then, while standing with your feet shoulder width apart, bring each leg up behind your back and grab your ankle. Pull your ankle toward your bum as much as possible into a standing quad stretch. With your feet in the same position, move into a hamstring stretch where you bend at the waist and try to touch your toes. You may want to spread your legs a little further and alternate between feet as you stretch over forward.

Next, you will move on to the upper body, starting with shoulder rolls. Again, stand with your feet shoulder-width apart and slowly swing your arms in circles. Gradually increase the size of the circles until you are coming close past your head on the way up and past your sides on the way down. Then, reverse the circle and repeat the process. This is a great way to ensure that your shoulders do not take undue strain from your pack during the hike. Next, move into a wrist stretch by interlocking your fingers and extending your arms directly ahead of yourself. Squeeze your elbows in and stretch as far as you can. Do this with your palms facing outward first and then with them facing inward. Wrist stretches are particularly important for more challenging hikes where you may need to grip rocks or branches to pull yourself up an incline.

Once you have completed your hike, it is a great idea to stretch again. This will allow your body to recuperate with less soreness or stiffness in the muscles and will shorten recovery time. The runner's lunge is a great post-hike stretch for the legs and you should alternate legs two or three times. Our legs will generally be the most tender area after a hike, so do not rush to complete these. Next, try the rag doll pose by holding onto the opposite elbow with each palm and spreading your legs. Then, bend over at the waist and gently sway from side to side. This is another great stretch for the legs as well as the spine. Lastly, place the toes of each foot on the ground and support your weight on the opposite leg. Roll your ankle in a circular motion at least 10 times going one way and then reverse. Do this up to three times. This is a great way to increase range of motion in the ankles, too, and can be a very beneficial stretch. In the following few days, notice where you hold any soreness and make an effort to focus your stretches on those areas in the future. Again, if at all unsure, please consult an expert.

Many other injuries are directly related to our gear and these can often be remedied very simply. No matter what the weather looks like as you set out from home, you should always be prepared for hot, cold, and wet conditions. We will look at hiking gear in a more in-depth way in the following chapter, but in terms of injury prevention, there are some important considerations. Firstly, hypothermia and hyperthermia are real risks when spending time on the trail, and our clothing is our first line of defense. It is fundamental that you understand the environment you are entering and know roughly what to expect. Always try to hike with as much of your body covered as possible. Lightweight and breathable material will keep you covered without making you excessively hot and this is generally preferable to sunscreen for the simple reason that you need not reapply. Having said that, always take sunscreen with you and apply to any exposed skin. The sun has an uncanny ability of finding our weak points and beating down on them. Also, always wear a hat even in overcast or rainy conditions. The sun is often at its most dangerous when it is unseen because we think it might be harmless. We have suffered our most savage sunburns on overcast days.

It is also always advisable to take a warm layer of clothing with you. Even if you hike all day with it weighing down your pack, you never want to find yourself in a situation where the cold blows in and shakes you to your core. Prioritize finding gear that is light but effective. Our last major source of injury on the trail is dehydration. Always take ample water, and again, it is better to be overprepared than dehydrated. While setting out with a heavy water-laden pack might be discouraging, there is nothing worse than becoming dizzy on the trail. Drink water regularly in small bursts. Drinking a little and often is preferable to drinking a lot of water whenever you stop for a break. Bear in mind that as you walk, this weight will decrease, and the better your levels of hydration, the easier the hike will be.

Hiking Techniques

Let's run through some ideas about different techniques you should bear in mind. Pace is the first major consideration. The old adage "slow and steady wins the race" applies here. It's important that you try to find the middle ground between speed and sustainability. It does you no good to race through the first few miles only to find yourself exhausted. Walking fast and then stopping often is going to tire you out in the long run. Find a pace that you can maintain for significant distances and try to stop infrequently. That being said, this is purely for your own enjoyment, so find what works best for you personally. You also want to be sure that your pack is not putting any unnecessary strain on your back or legs. Adjusting your pack might seem like a minor detail, but it can make a massive difference to your level of comfort on the trail. Pull your straps as tight as you can comfortably manage. It should not be moving around much on your back as you walk. This will help you avoid rashes while putting as little pressure on your back, neck, and shoulders as possible. Day packs are generally smaller and should be close to the nape of your neck.

Stretching is also an important technique that will improve your comfort both on the trails and immediately afterward. We've been through a number of important stretches above, but remember to adapt these to suit your style. Breaks are also an important factor on the trails. Try to keep them as short as possible, especially on longer hikes. We generally keep our breaks shorter than 10 minutes, as this allows us to maintain momentum and motivation. Sitting around for extended periods will make it far harder to get going again. You should also aim to make your breaks effective. Drink some water and perhaps have a bite of an apple on all your breaks, but do not overindulge. By doing so, you will be able to easily resume the trail feeling hydrated and fueled. On a dawn to dusk hike, you will need to stop for lunch at some point and this should also be kept short. Try to break for less than 30 minutes for lunch. We always feel a post-lunch dip in energy levels, and the quicker you get going again, the less this will affect you.

Our next point may seem silly, but you need to think about your walking technique. Everyone thinks they know how to walk; after all, it's one of the first things we learn to do. However, poor form can seriously increase the risk of injury or pain on the trails. Everyone has a slightly different perspective, but humans are biologically wired to walk by landing on the heel of the foot and then rolling our weight forward through the arch and bouncing off the foot's ball. Many of us have lost this natural rhythm in our stride, and if you find yourself in this category, try to correct yourself before you incur any painful penalties. Always walk with your back straight and move in consistent and comfortable ways. Lean into your back and allow it to correct your posture because slouching on a hike is going to cause you back problems in the future.

The last consideration we want to introduce is the difference in walking uphill and downhill. This, again, is a contentious topic with every hiker having a slightly different take. In any lengthy hike, there will be ups and downs interspersed with level walking. This makes hiking a very effective workout, as each of these works slightly different muscles, and combining them is a great way to ensure a well-rounded exercise. It is important to adjust your technique slightly through these changes. On downhill sections you can relax a little and flow with your body's natural momentum. Take bigger strides and simply allow gravity to do the rest. Try to maintain a straight posture and step deliberately. Additionally, try to slow your pace slightly as your body weight will make up this difference. When a path gets steep, try to take it sideways, and always take care to test the ground in treacherous terrain before committing your weight.

With uphill sections, you should try to take shorter strides but slightly more frequently. Do not exhaust yourself by taking very short strides at a much faster rate. Rather, shorten your stride slightly while maintaining your pace. Lean into the hill slightly but maintain a straight back. Also, try to lower the height of your knees as you walk. Taking shorter strides should lend itself toward this, but making the effort will decrease the level of strain and allow you to move at a steady pace. Again, add variety until you find what works well for you personally, but bear these tips in mind. The most important point here is to pay attention to your body. If you experience any pain or discomfort, take the steps to work them out before they become serious hindrances. Your hiking technique can either really improve your enjoyment of the trails or end your interest. It might take a little trial and error, but you will get there.

Chapter 2:

Choosing the Right Gear

Gear is something we underestimate at our own peril. It might seem an insignificant detail, but everything from the material of your shirt to the cut of your pants is going to affect how you hike. In this chapter, we are going to look at different options you have when selecting the perfect equipment for your needs. Our gear is our first line of defense against injury, the elements, and unpreparedness. When selecting clothes and accessories for a hike, it is almost as important to know what you do not need as what you do. Whatever you take with you is going to weigh you down and so you need to find a balance between utility and movability. We have taken unnecessary extras on hikes and neglected important items. The results of these exploits have varied from mild irritation to real regret. Hopefully, after reading this chapter, you won't make the same mistakes.

Clothing

Never underestimate the importance of the right clothes on the trail. The right clothing can mean the difference between finishing a long hike with a sense of achievement and completing it miserably covered in blisters, sunburned, and disheartened. So, let's take a look at how to ensure you have the best items of clothing for your needs. Broadly, we can break a hiking outfit down into several important categories: footwear, socks, shirts, pants, headwear, and jackets. Each needs to be considered before setting out on the trails. Before we get into each one, some general advice: Avoid denim and cotton at all costs! These materials will lock in all the sweat you release on the hike and ensure you carry it all with you. Sweat-wicking is essentially a material's ability to draw liquids to its outer surface where it dries or dissipates but does not soak the material itself. This is a vital quality you should look for in your hiking attire, otherwise you run the risk of severe discomfort and rash outbreaks as well as being far more susceptible to weather changes. Opt for light breathable materials wherever possible.

It is worth mentioning that you may want to consider the effect underwear has as well. We recommend nylon or polyester. With underwear, you need to consider support, comfort, and coverage. These materials are stretchy and comfortable while still supporting you where it's important. Underwear branded for exercise will generally treat you well. When considering shirts and pants, you should consider comfort, stretch, sweat-wicking, strength, durability, and warmth. Traditionally, the following materials are used for active wear: lycra, polyester, nylon, cotton, and polypropylene. Shirts can be a little more forgiving but you may want to wear pants over shorts generally. You never know what kind of plants you may trek through and so it is always a good idea to have slightly better lower leg coverage. You might want to experiment and find what works best, but remember that cotton is very absorbent and will hold moisture, giving the other materials a slight edge. Lycra is less strong and durable than the rest and so you might want to build the majority of your outdoor wardrobe out of nylon, polyester, and polypropylene. These are the best in terms of stretch, comfort, durability, and sweat-wicking. Their one downside is that they are not very warm, which leads us to jerseys and jackets.

If you are planning to spend an entire day on a trail, you need to be prepared for a variety of conditions. The weather can turn on a dime and you need to prepare for this. Always prioritize lightweight materials so that if you do end up carrying your jacket the whole day, it does not add much strain. There are three main types of waterproof jacket. These are: wax-coated, PU-coated (polyurethane), and membrane lined jackets. Wax-coated jackets are a little old fashioned and require maintenance. They are also generally rather heavy and not very breathable. For these reasons, we recommend either PU-coated or membrane-lined jackets. Both of these can be nicely breathable and lightweight. We always recommend a waterproof jacket as you can never be sure when rain will threaten a hike.

Aside from the construction, consider the following aspects carefully before any purchase: Does the jacket have a hood? If it does not, you will run the risk of funneling water down the back of your neck and backside. This is really not great for longer hikes and you should try to have some kind of head covering. What kind of pockets does the jacket have? If you are going to walk in the rain, you need to ensure your possessions stay dry. Look for jackets that have waterproof zips or internal pockets. You may also want to consider pocket placement. If your pockets are out of reach when you are wearing your pack, then maybe look a little farther. Also consider the front zip of the jacket. Look for items that ensure waterproofing either with good zip technology or with an adjustable covering. It is infuriating to have a dry back but a wet front as you walk. Lastly, does the jacket have any kind of venting? Many jackets these days are built with zips in the armpits and sometimes on the back. This is great for cold weather when it is not raining. You want to ensure that you can be dry in a pinch but a little more open when necessary. If you are hiking in very cold conditions, take an extra layer. Wool is a great breathable material that will help you stay warm without weighing you down.

Let's move down the body to our feet. Socks can be really important on a hike but are so often underestimated. There are four main points to consider when choosing the perfect pair of socks. Think about the height, fabric, cushioning, and fit. In terms of height, choose according to your shoe. Always try to have your socks end above the line of your shoe, otherwise you will risk them sliding down and bunching at the bottom. The crew cut is a classic hiking level sock. This ends generally halfway up the calf and is compatible with all kinds of shoes and boots. If you are unsure, err on the side of caution and get these. In colder weather, knee-high socks will add an element of warmth. In hotter weather, you may want shorter socks to ensure you do not overheat. When thinking about cushioning, again consider your shoes. If you are walking on a hot day, consider socks with light cushioning. This will increase comfort without the threat of overheating. In colder weather, go for something with heavier cushioning. Heavy-cushioned socks will keep you warm and comfortable but may slow you down on hot days. If you are simply looking for good all-round socks for a variety of conditions, opt for medium cushioning, as these are more versatile and forgiving.

When thinking about fabrics, we recommend wool, nylon, or polyester. These are all great wicking materials and are durable and hold their shape. The ideal sock is a wool blend, as these are naturally breathable, good sweat-wickers and have the added benefit of being antimicrobial for less odor. Lastly, get socks that fit snugly without being tight. This means you should get socks for your specific foot size, as they will not shift during the hike and will help prevent blistering. It is worth noting that your foot size and shoe size may differ slightly, so some trying out might be beneficial.

Shoes are an incredibly important piece of gear for any hiker. The first consideration, and perhaps most obvious, is the fit. You need to get shoes that fit you properly. Footwear that is too big or small is a recipe for blisters no matter how effective your socks may be. That being said, there are a number of great options when thinking about footwear. Your main options are sandals, trail running shoes, low-cut, and high-cut boots. If you predominantly hike in a hot climate, sandals may be your best bet. These are always very breathable but have less support. If you are doing longer hikes, you may want to choose something a little more sturdy. Trail running shoes generally have great outsoles for traction but also lack ankle support. Your gear will depend heavily on your style of hiking. If you are moving fast and carrying as little as possible, trail runners may be for you. We typically recommend ankle-cut boots. If you are going for this heavier style of shoe, you might as well add that level of stability in the ankle. This will help you to prevent sprains and add a level of protection against plants, critters, and water.

Finally, the makeup of your shoes is important. The main components are the boot uppers (or materials), the midsoles (or cushion), the internal support, and the outsoles (or grip). In terms of uppers, you will again need to consider your hiking goals. If you are looking to do mild intensity day hiking over fair terrain, it is not necessary to get heavy full-grain leather boots. Consider split-grain boots for their breathability and lighter buildup. If you are looking at more strenuous trails through variable terrain, it is better to be more prepared. Look at either full-grain leather (or a vegan alternative) or membrane waterproofing. These options will be less breathable but will keep your feet dry through streams and swampy conditions.

Midsoles should be firm but comfortable. When looking at multiple day trips, you may want to go stiffer, but for day hiking, a mild stiffness will do nicely. You can always supplement this with a slip-in insole if you find the midsole too stiff or forgiving. Lastly, when looking at outsoles, you should consider two main factors: lug pattern and heel brake. The lug pattern is simply the way the grip on the shoe's bottom is set out. A lug is a single traction-giving bump and these can be set out in a variety of ways. Essentially, look at the pattern of grip nodules at the base of the shoe as well as the heel section. Deeper grooves between the lugs and a tighter gap is going to improve grip while broader spacing is good for traction and will shed mud more easily. You may need the tighter, grippier formation if you are hoping to move into multiple day hiking, but otherwise, a bigger spacing will make your shoes more lightweight without sacrificing too much stability and grip. The heel brake refers to the pattern on the back of the shoe. This is generally a distinct heel section that differs from the rest of the lug pattern. These are usually separated by the arch of a boot or shoe but not all hiking boots have them. A heel brake is a great way to ensure you have better traction on steeper slopes. Keep an eye out for boots with a substantial heel brake. This will decrease your risk of slipping when navigating steeper terrain. If you are looking at very mild hikes, then this is less important. The most fundamental point here is that you should know what conditions and level you will generally be hiking through and cater to those requirements.

Bags

The trusty day pack is very important and you should invest in something strong and durable. Always get a backpack. There is a time and a place for a duffel bag or rucksack but it is not on a hiking trail. You will absolutely need two free hands to navigate treacherous terrain or even simply take photos. For day trekking, a simple frameless backpack will do nicely, although there are still some aspects to consider. You are going to need something adjustable. Packs that do not have adjustable straps are only going to wear you down on the trail. Unless they are somehow tailored to your body, they will shift around and move the weight back and forth on your back. This will result in soreness in your spine and perhaps rashes on the line of the bottom of the pack. Keep your pack tight to your back and ensure you can adjust it where necessary. If you are taking a heavier pack, you may want to consider something with hip straps. Again, ensure that these are adjustable. These can balance the load bearing between your back and hips and allow for added stability and support. If you are planning a dawn to dusk hike, this may be a better option as you do not want to contribute to any future back pain.

Next, you should consider storage, volume, and additional pockets or compartments. Think about all the things you will be taking along on your hike (see the checklist in Bonuses for some ideas). If you are a more specialized hobbyist, like a photographer or landscape painter, take this into consideration as well and think about a specialist pack. Some staples that you should definitely have are a jacket, ample water, sunscreen, food, a first aid kit, and perhaps a knife or multi-tool, such as a Swiss Army knife. Daypacks generally only hold around 10–14 kgs. This should be more than enough space for any intrepid day trekker.

Make sure that you can fit all of your stables into the main body of the bag and ideally have side storage options for water bottles. Being able to easily access your water will cut your stoppage time and allow you to hydrate steadily on the go. Compartments and pockets also allow you to organize your items and keep certain items apart. You definitely don't want to keep your leaky sunscreen bottle next to your food! It is always a great idea to have a trial pack before any big hike to ensure that all your items will fit. When you pack, do so in order of lowest to highest priority. On a hot day, pack your jacket at the bottom and your sunscreen on top. This is another good way to streamline stoppage times. You may also want separate storage for items such as your house keys and mobile phone. A pocket for your most valuable items is always a great idea, as you do not want to risk accidentally tossing them out while searching for something else.

Lastly, you should consider the material used and the conditions you will subject the pack to. We always recommend a pack with a ventilated mesh back and straps. This ensures you will not get unduly hot on your back and will walk more comfortably. While ventilation is not strictly necessary for shorter distances, it will always add a level of comfort. In colder conditions you may find this unnecessary, as your pack will rest against your jacket. Again, always focus these decisions around your needs. You should also think about waterproofing. Many packs are not waterproof but come with covers that are. If you are doing full day hikes, this is an absolute must-have. You never want to be in a position where everything you have with you gets soaked. Unless you live in the desert, it is better to have some kind of waterproofing solution.

Sticks/Walking Poles

One, two, none? What are hiking poles and when should you use them? Well, this is very person-dependent and the hiking community has not reached a clear consensus on the issue. This is something else you need to decipher for yourself. Hiking poles are walking sticks generally made from carbon fiber, aluminum, or a combination of the two. They are lightweight and often have comfortable handles molded to the shape of a hand and a wrist strap. They are generally sold in a set of two, although some hikers favor just one pole. Let's take a look at some reasons to use them and some reasons not to.

Hiking poles are an effective way to take the weight off your knees. Using two hiking poles is a great way to give your knees and ankles some respite on the trail. This is especially helpful on trickier descents or ascents. You will also find that poles ensure a full body workout on the trails. If we just let our arms hang at our sides for an entire day out, they may swell slightly as a result of poor circulation. Poles allow you to avoid this by ensuring that your arms are not only moving, but working. This also encourages a consistent rhythm in your movements and may help you to keep a steady pace. They also help us balance, and if you often find yourself slipping on hikes, then maybe this is a great investment to consider. We use poles every hike just for that added knee support. You might consider doing the same if you are at all concerned about your knees.

If you find yourself longing for more complex or lengthy hiking, poles have a few more benefits. They are a safe means of testing treacherous terrain, from loose sand on a slope to ice thickness and water depths. We definitely recommend poles to anyone doing multi-day hiking for the simple reason that you won't have to put your body on the line to discover the safest path forward. You might also need them to throw together an impromptu shelter or bivouac. If you are wanting to expand your range, a pair of hiking poles can support a tarp or covering and will be simpler and sturdier than finding sticks. Lastly, they can act as a last line of defense if you find yourself in a dangerous interaction with an animal. We definitely do not recommend fighting wildlife with hiking poles, but should you find yourself flung into a confrontation beyond your control, you may be glad to have your poles. They will allow you to clear snakes, spiders, and scorpions from a path at a safe distance and can be banged together or waved to discourage the approach of bigger animals. Wildlife varies depending on where you are planning on hiking. If you are entering a space with wild animals, you may want to carry poles for increased peace of mind.

There are, of course, some downsides to poles. If you are doing technical hiking that requires you to support yourself with your hands, you are going to be putting the poles away constantly and taking them out again. This can be annoying and will also add weight to your pack for technical stretches of the trail. They also might tire you out quicker than walking without them. While you are getting a fuller workout, you are also working harder to cover the same distance. This can be very unappealing to certain hikers. Lastly, if you are a hobbyist, like a photographer or birdwatcher, you are going to be juggling your poles with your camera or binoculars. This can be very off-putting, especially if you are trying to get a quick shot on the move.

For full day hiking, we really only recommend poles if you need the added support when balancing or if you need to take the pressure off of your knees. Poles will serve you very well in these cases. However, if these issues don't really affect you, you probably won't need poles until you begin to venture into multi-day hiking territory. That being said, not all poles are made the same. While they are generally made from similar lightweight material, their construction can differ massively. We always recommend extendable poles that either have telescopic extensions or a trifold setup. Telescopic poles will extend by fitting into each other and can be extended or collapsed very easily. A trifold setup generally consists of three sections of pole with a tension cord attaching them that can be pulled taught to form a sturdy hiking pole. These two designs have the edge over fixed poles, as they are far lighter and easier to transport without compromising stability in a major way.

Our last piece of advice is to make sure you get the right sized poles. When you are gripping the handles and standing up straight, your elbow should be at a 90° angle. Poles that are too short are going to see you hunch over on the trails and put a lot more strain on your back. Poles that are too tall are going to push your posture backwards, resulting in more shoulder and lower back strain. If you are going to use poles, get comfortable with them first and walk around your house with them a few times, although be careful not to scuff your floor!

Rain Gear

Rain is a constant threat on the trails. You are definitely going to want to be prepared for sudden showers while hiking. We've covered this a little above, but the important points are worth reiterating. Waterproofing can be divided into two categories, namely waterproofing yourself and your gear. Let's take a look at both of these. Firstly, when thinking of yourself, a waterproof rain jacket is a must. There are many lightweight options that use PU-coats or are membrane lined, and you should definitely invest in something like this. Keeping your upper body and items like mobile phones and car keys dry is vital. There's no way to get around it, you need a raincoat.

Your legs are a little less important, although there are a number of products out there that will keep you dry here too. It is important at this point to note that products can be labeled slightly differently and this has a big impact. Waterproof items will not allow any moisture to pass through the outer layer, with the inverse effect being a locking in of sweat. Water-resistant items are more breathable and will guard against becoming soaked if you are splashed or exposed to mild precipitation. Lastly, you will find items that are marked quick-dry. These are not waterproof at all but can be dried out very quickly. These are great for hot weather hikes where you may cross streams or stop for a swim.

Again, the weather is going to be a huge factor in what you choose. If you are hiking in colder conditions, always opt for the maximum waterproofing, as any wetness is going to get very cold very quickly. In hotter climates, try to use your discretion. In drier areas, you may wish to simply take quick dry items such as shirts and shorts. In a dry heat you can cross water, or even swim and simply allow these to dry out as you walk. You are also at lower risk of rain. In more humid conditions where the air is heavy with moisture, you are still going to want breathable material, but perhaps opt for water resistant clothing, as you will not dry out as you walk. If rain does surprise you, you can keep relatively dry without overheating. You would be surprised at how unpleasant a hot and humid climate can be if you are soaked.

In terms of footwear, the colder your chosen trail, the more important it is that you have waterproof boots. In warmer weather, consider your options a little more carefully. Fully waterproof boots are going to lock in that heat and make walking slightly more arduous. Water resistant boots are probably more ideal, although these may become soaked and a real burden if you are constantly crossing streams or trekking in steady rain. If it is safe to do so, remove your shoes and socks before mild water crossings to ensure your shoes stay dry. If you can do this, water-resistant boots will serve you perfectly. If you are walking in warm conditions with many water crossings or mild precipitation, your best bet may be hiking sandals. These will allow you to simply walk without worrying about taking your footwear off for crossings. Always consider the conditions first and then make your decisions.

Let's move on to gear. For day hiking, your main concern is going to be your pack. It is possible to find completely waterproof daypacks, although these will generally test the budget a little. For guarding against rain, a simple waterproof pack covering will do you well. Look for packs that come with these, as this will ensure a snug fit. If you already have a pack, it is possible to buy these separately or even improvise one, although we do not recommend this. This is by far the best way to keep your pack dry. Some hikers have oversized jackets that fit over their packs. This might work, although it is going to leave room for you to get cold when you are wearing the jacket without the pack. If your pack and upper body are dry, you should be able to manage any rainy hike in relative comfort. One last consideration is taking an umbrella. If you are going to do this, ensure you have a lightweight and compact one that can fit comfortably in your pack. This may prove a godsend on particularly wet days but absolutely never take it out if there is lightning around.

We were once caught in a heavy downpour at the furthest possible point in the trail from our car. It was at this moment that we realized only one of us had remembered a waterproof jacket. We had forgotten one at home, and although we toyed with the idea of alternating the jacket, this would have simply ruined both our days. We were on a very open trail and we realized there was no real option for finding cover anywhere near us. We ended up half-jogging around eight kilometers back to the car in the bucketing rain. Once safely in the heated car, the benefit of the jacket was clearly apparent. One of us was dry above the waist and in good spirits while the other was drenched to the bone and grumbling as if the world was ending. Learn from us and try to be a little more prepared than we were that day.

First Aid

A first aid kit is an absolute must-have for any hiker. These are vital to safety and managing dangerous situations. Let's go through some items you need and why they are important. Firstly, you need to be able to patch up any wounds that may be inflicted on you or your fellow hikers. You are going to want to have some bandages, gauze, medical tape, and antiseptic wipes. These are going to be very important in the case of a fall or bumps and scrapes. Out on the trails, you will need to immediately sanitize the wound with antiseptic wipes. This is preferable to having a bottle of antiseptic solution as wipes are easier to carry and also ensure an even distribution. You will then be able to wrap up the wound and either continue or call for aid. Ensure that you have enough bandages and gauze to cater to bigger wounds and stem blood flow. Ideally, you will never actually need these but you must always be prepared for worst-case scenarios.

Medical tape is great for smaller cuts and scrapes although you should always sanitize the area before applying anything further. Infections can be a seriously nasty and potentially very dangerous result of a fall. You may want to carry an adjustable splint, too, in case of broken bones or fractures. This is a great idea, as improvising one from a nearby stick can exacerbate the break. In this case, you need to call for proper medical assistance as quickly as possible. Always have your mobile phone with you on a hike. You may get spotty reception on the trails but on day hikes you should be able to reach coverage to call for help.

Next, you are going to want to carry painkillers, antihistamines, tweezers, and ointment for insect stings. Painkillers can be a great help in the case of a more serious incident but can also allow you to keep moving if you get a sudden headache or migraine. When on the trails, you never know what is going to spark your allergies. Antihistamines can generally calm these symptoms and allow you to continue in relative comfort. Tweezers can help you to deal with minor injuries like splinters or thorns. You may want to carry a needle, too, for cases like bee stings where tweezers will simply break the venom sack and worsen the sting. Please note, if you are allergic to bees or anything you are likely to encounter on a hike, you need to be prepared with antivenoms or epipens. Lastly, an ointment for insect stings or plant poisons is a great item to carry. If you are not well versed in plant life, it is very easy to walk through poison ivy and the like. While this can be a minor injury, without intervention it will become far worse. Treating insect stings should also be a priority, as this is a common trail injury.

Lastly, you need to be prepared for irritations as well as more serious incidents. Items like bug spray, sunscreen, lip balm, feminine hygiene products, and a space blanket for cold weather hikes are all crucial. They may seem more obvious, but prevention is always better than a cure. Bug sprays are commonly general insecticides and can ensure that you discourage insects from targeting you and will protect against mosquitoes, bees, and wasps. Please take care though because you simply want to protect yourself and should not be killing insects wantonly in their natural habitat. Sunscreen is an absolute must-have for any weather. Even in very cold weather, your exposed skin may be chapped and blistered by the sun. Always protect yourself against this. Lip balm is another must-have simply to ensure that your lips don't become chapped. This may seem minor but it is always better to be prepared. Feminine hygiene products are always great to include if you are in a mixed group of hikers. While women are generally prepared for this, you never know when someone may need a pad in a pinch. If you plan on hiking in cold weather, you need to have a space blanket. They are very light and compact and can mean the difference between life and death on an unplanned night out in the cold.

Other Useful Items

These next items may not be essential but they may still be of great help to you in a variety of situations. Many hikers like to carry a knife or multitool on the trails. This may be more useful for longer multi-day trips, but even on full day hikes they can be useful. If you find yourself in an emergency situation and you have to spend the night on a trail, a knife can be really useful for setting up a bivouac. This will allow you to safely cut branches and fashion twines from the plant life around you. Multitools are recommended, as a pair of pliers, tweezers, a can opener, and bottle opener have a wider applicability than a simple knife. It is important to note that carrying a knife is not always legal and you should be sure of the legislation in your area before packing one.

Next, a headlamp or flashlight may be a very clever idea. For full day hikes, you always run the risk of returning after dark. Headlights in particular are very effective, as these allow you to remain aware of your surroundings with two free hands. This may seem like an unnecessary extra that just weighs you down, but if you are planning to be back just before sunset, take one along. It is always best to err on the side of caution when it comes to walking in the pitch dark. You may also be forced to spend a night on the trail in an emergency. In a case like this, you will need a source of light to illuminate your area but also to attract attention.

Finally, you may want to take a camera. While far from essential, a camera allows you to look at the world around you differently. We always carry a camera because our surroundings are simply too beautiful to not capture. It is important that you remember why you hike. The beauty of this activity is that it puts us in incredible spaces and a camera will often remind us to take it all in. On a dawn to dusk hike, you will have the added benefit of two separate "golden hours." While this is not for everyone, it will allow you to remember moments better. Often, we cannot simply sit and drink in our surroundings for as long as we want, and in these cases, snapping a photograph is a great compromise.

Women and Children Specific Gear

We are not trying to suggest that women are any less effective hikers than men. There are, however, some differences that are worth noting. Visiting the restroom is one such concern. Men are lucky in this regard, as it is a simple operation of stepping off the trail. For women, this is slightly more complex. A reusable toilet paper alternative is a great gear addition that reduces trail waste and adds comfort to the process. Many alternatives are available and you should simply take a little extra water for a rinse and squeeze. Women also need to consider their menstrual cycle, and so packing hygiene products such as tampons or pads is ideal. Prepare accordingly based on your personal cycle. We actually encourage both men and women to carry pads. This is not only a considerate gesture, but pads can also act as an effective gauze substitute and are naturally effective at soaking up blood in an emergency. Scientists have shown that men and women are equally effective hikers and do not suffer any injuries disproportionately. Simple biological differences are the only major consideration here.

That being said, there are a number of items that are beneficial to women on a hike. Firstly, upper body support. Sports bras are far superior to any regular wear bras on a hike. They have much better support and will prevent back pain to an extent. Hiking can be a high-impact sport, especially as you progress to harder trails, and so a sports bra is essential. Women should avoid cotton underwear and try to find effective wicking or quick-dry materials. In terms of outfits, we recommend more stretchable or adjustable items for women. Leggings can be a great benefit on the trail, as they are very comfortable and help you to avoid chafing as you walk. It is important that you find gear that fits you well and is also comfortable. Leggings offer a better range of motion than other hiking pants, but take care to find well-constructed pairs that are reinforced in critical areas. This will ensure the longevity of the leggings too.

Women may also want to consider their packs a little more carefully. Find something that fits your shape well. You do not want a pack to hang too low on your back and chafe around the hips. While there are many unisex options, women's packs are generally tailored to better fit necks, backs, and hips. This can make all the difference on a hike, as these added features will help you to walk comfortably and avoid strain injuries. Try to find an ergonomic and breathable option that fits your shape well. Also prioritize adjustable gear. We all change over time, and gear that can adjust to fit our changing physiques will be a great investment as you progress through your hiking career.

If you are hiking with your children, you need to take steps to ensure their safety. Lengthy hiking trails are often tough on little legs and you should be certain your child can manage the strain. If you are sure your child is ready and eager for a hike, there are some tips you might consider. Start on easier and shorter trails. Do not throw your child into the proverbial deep end. Rather, start small and work your way onto more challenging hikes. It is also important to ensure that your kids are stimulated. Try to start with hikes that have features your children will find interesting such as trees to climb or a lake. This is a great way to ensure your children enjoy the experience and will encourage a continuation of this hobby. Remember that your children are going to need to stop more often and you should pack plenty of snacks and water.

In terms of gear, your children should be as prepared as you are. Ensure they have adequate clothing and take care to apply sunscreen and bug spray as needed. If you do not want to carry all of your children's food and supplies, consider getting them a pack of their own. A small and lightweight pack that allows them to carry their own water is ideal. In doing so, you will give your children some responsibility on the trails and allow them to drink independently when they need to. A hydration pack may be a great idea, as they will be able to drink on the move through a nozzle. It is also very important that your children have adequate footwear. Parents often get items for their children that they "will grow into." Unfortunately, on the trails this is a bad idea. Get your children shoes that fit them properly. Children have more sensitive feet than adults and so it is very important that they are adequately comfortable and supportive. This will mean several new pairs of shoes as your children grow, but it will be worth it in terms of keeping them safe and stable.

You may also want to consider child specific hats and other items for assisting your child. Children need sun protection, and drawstring wide brim hats are a great way to ensure that their hats stay on and provide a good deal of coverage. Be careful to apply sunscreen regularly too. For younger children, you might consider a carrier pack as well, which allows you to carry your children with free hands. Encourage your children to walk as much as possible, but if they become exhausted, this may be a great item to have on hand. Also consider a harness and leash, for younger children, if you are planning on going anywhere near hazardous areas. Sharp precipices and large bodies of water can be a parent's worst nightmare, but a firm handle on your children will allow them to explore in relative freedom while maintaining your peace of mind.

Our final point is that this chapter is not a limitless resource. We always recommend speaking to the assistants at your local outdoor shop and getting their advice on the gear you need. They will be able to give you much more personal advice and should find you the best gear for your purposes and proposed trail. It is always great to lean on the expertise of others when getting started, and this begins with gear. Ensure you have everything you need and that it fits you well.

Chapter 3:

Choosing a Route

Now that you're fit enough and have kitted yourself out with the right gear, let's look at choosing the right hike. In this chapter, we will go through all the ins and outs of selecting a hike, creating and sticking to an itinerary, and arranging permits. This is a really exciting step and will allow you to start hiking with confidence. Bear in mind that these tips may vary depending on where you live or hope to hike. You will always need to do research on your chosen trail, but we will show you how and the right questions to ask. Take on hikes at your level and try to work toward harder and longer hikes rather than attempting challenging trails off the bat. This process is neither a sprint nor a marathon; it is the start of a journey. Work gradually and play to your strengths. Hiking is all about absorbing the beauty around us and breaking the barriers between us and the natural world. You cannot do this overnight but you can take steps consistently that will ensure that you progress steadily and are able to meet your hiking goals. Let's dive in.

The Hike

There is a lot to think about when planning a hike. The coming tips are more important for your first one because this will set the tone going forward. Everyone remembers their very first hike. We'll try to make sure you remember it with fondness and not regret. Our biggest tip is to start small. Look for trails near your house that are of entry-level to mild difficulty. It's always great to get multiple perspectives in this process, as many of the difficulties are set by veteran hikers who may underestimate certain trails. If you know any hikers, ask them to recommend some beginner-friendly trails. For your first few hikes, you should also try to find circular trails that start where they end. We will look at linear trails in more detail further on, but for starters, try to find a route that comes back to the start. This just minimizes coordination and gives you the benefit of being able to double back should it prove too much. Many hiking trails are given a difficulty rating. In North America, trails will generally be given a rating out of three, with one being the easiest and three the most challenging. In Europe, this varies a little. There may be a rating scale out of five, with one being the easiest, or the trail may be described as easy, intermediate, or challenging. South Africa uses a rating system, too, although a slightly different one. South African hikes are attributed to one of the following numbers: 0, 1, 2, 2+, 3, 4. The easiest trail here is a 0, while a hike with a rating of 4 will be very strenuous and constantly require scrambling over rocks. Wherever you find yourself in the world, be sure of the rules and ratings of the hikes you attempt. Always start on trails with a rating of one if at all possible.

Another important aspect to consider is the features of a hike. Especially in the beginning, try to find a trail that appeals to you. Find a trail that features a waterfall, beautiful forest, or lake if any of these appeal to you. Hiking is compatible with a whole host of other hobbies such as photography, bird and wildlife watching, and swimming. If you have a hobby that you already really enjoy, try to link it to the hiking trails. If you love swimming, then perhaps find a trail that leads to a lake before doubling back. Be careful to prepare adequately and take a change of clothes and something to carry the wet ones in. You do not want to hike half a trail in wet gear!

Next you want to consider the distance and elevation. As we've said, it is far better to work up to more challenging hikes. As you start out, try to strike a balance between these that suits your level of fitness and goals. Start with hikes that are shorter distances and have lower elevation gains. Even if you think you are very fit, start with something a little less challenging. This is a great way to gauge your actual hiking fitness. If you find the first one easy, then begin to aim higher and further. Note that short hikes with heavy elevations are going to take you longer than you think. It is also common for flatter hiking trails to be branded as beginner friendly, even though they might cover longer distances. While you will often find these hikes manageable, start with something shorter.

Also consider the conditions. If you live in a colder region, the higher elevations are going to mean a sharp temperature drop and an increased likelihood of snow and ice. In the beginning, these are treacherous obstacles that you should try to avoid to as great an extent as possible. Once you are more confident, then start to find more obstacle-intensive trails. If you live in a hot area, consider exposure and shade on the hike. To start out with, you should aim to do a good portion of your walking in the shade. Always prepare for harsh sun, but if your first hike is through blistering heat the entire time, you may be put off. Look for trails that feature a forest so that you know you can walk in comfort.

When thinking about elevation gain and distance, you must also think about the time you have available. Many hiking trails have estimated times for completion. We recommend that you give yourself more time than required, especially for your first few hikes. If a particular trail has an estimated completion time of around two hours (a good starting time), give yourself at least three just in case. This will allow you to take the trail at your own pace, while also allowing you a margin for error if the hike is more challenging than you think. This is generally good practice for more experienced hikers too. Often, we take longer breaks and walk at a slower place than we think we will. An itinerary is a great way to motivate yourself and ensure you have enough time to complete the trail. Set out a rough time guide for yourself and be sure to include stoppage time. Try to stick to the timings you set out as best as possible, although do not be disheartened if you cannot. So often a trail is more challenging than we think and this can be a real source of dejection among beginners.

The more research you do beforehand, the better you will find the hike. Many online resources will outline seasonal differences on the trail and you should take note. In colder climates, an easy trail in summer may become very hazardous in winter. On the other hand, in warmer climates, an easy winter trail may be too hot in summer. These may seem somewhat insignificant, but on the trail these distinctions can be vital. You need to know what kind of terrain you will be dealing with too. Soft sand, for example, is a lot less passable than harder surfaces and even moderate hikes will sap your energy. Train for the landscapes you will take on and try to practice walking on similar surfaces if you are able. You should also prepare for potential obstacles in your path. You may have to navigate fallen trees, climbing sections, or river crossings. If you understand what you will face ahead of time, you can prepare yourself physically and in terms of your gear.

If you are taking on a linear trail, there is going to be an element of logistical planning that you need to address. You will have to either park at the end and find transport to the start or vice versa. Some trails, particularly in national parks, have an option to organize transport through the operating body. Where this is not possible, you need to organize something yourself. In the beginning we always recommend that you hike with at least one other person. This will serve to motivate you as well as making the whole experience more enjoyable and social. If you cannot find a partner, be sure to take careful note of the next section. If you have a hiking partner, you can also drive in convoy to the end of the hike and drop a car there before heading to the beginning. This is probably the easiest way to deal with a linear trail. Before setting out, you need to be certain of the trail's route. Finding yourself on a linear trail that you assumed was circular is a recipe for disaster.

One last consideration is in regard to your group or companions. If you are hiking with a dog, you need to make sure that the trail is pet friendly. Make sure you understand the rules of the trail before embarking. Some trails may allow dogs only on a leash, while others may allow dogs to walk along freely. Some trails do not allow dogs at all. When walking with a dog, try to be considerate of your fellow hikers and keep your pet close beside you or on a leash if they tend to wander. Always pay attention to the rules and ensure your compliance. You will also need to take some extras, such as bags to pick up after your dog and a water bowl. You should also consider the features, as rivers and sharp precipices can be very hazardous for dogs. If you are hiking with a child, terrain is also going to be a huge factor. Slight inclines may be easy for most adults but impassable for children. Always choose the easiest hike possible when trekking with a youngster and be wary of the fact that you may end up carrying them for sections (especially with younger children and toddlers). The best piece of advice when selecting your first hike is to overestimate everything. Give yourself more time than is recommended and prepare for all types of terrain you may encounter. There are no consequences for being overprepared, while there may well be if you are not prepared enough.

So, now that you know what to consider when choosing a hike, where can you look for them? This will again vary depending on your location, but national park websites or offices are always a great place to start. Generally, national parks employees will be very knowledgeable of the trails and can make great recommendations. You might also simply run a Google search and see what comes up for your area. If you are going to Google some hikes, it may be a good idea to read any reviews you can to see how others found the hike and if they have any tips or concerns. Social media can also be a useful tool for finding trails in your area. Follow and subscribe to some hiking accounts and see if they share any helpful tips or recommendations. If you know of anyone who is into hiking, ask them too. There is no substitute for experience and so asking others can be a really great way to find out about hidden gems or manageable trails. Conversations like these may also lead you to groups or societies of hikers who may offer insight into trails to take on or even have group activities that you could participate in. However you choose to proceed, ensure that you do the research and are sure of yourself and the trail.

Keeping Safe as a Solo Walker

Sometimes it isn't possible to find a reliable hiking partner. This is no reason to give up altogether—it just requires a little more preparation. Most of this will read like common sense advice, but take note regardless. It is very important that you give yourself even more leeway on hikes if you are attempting them by yourself. Give yourself a little more time on the trail and leave a bit earlier to ensure you do not return in the dark. Again, it is vital that you understand the trail you will be taking and are ready for the terrain. You need to take extra care when alone, as help will not be as readily available. It is also very important that you do not take any unnecessary risks when you are by yourself. If a section looks too steep or a river crossing too deep, go around. If it is impossible to go around, consider backtracking and finding an alternate route. In groups, we can always assist each other and minimize risks, whereas solo, this is not always possible.

Again, choose your trail carefully and read weather forecasts. Take all necessary weather gear with you and make sure you know where you are going. Group mishaps can become very dangerous when you are alone and you might consider postponing if there is rain or heavy wind. You should also take a map and a compass. This is good practice for any hiker but doubly so when you are by yourself. As well, this is simply some added risk management, and if you do get lost, you can find your way back safely. Ensure that you understand how to read a map and operate a compass before taking them on the trail, as you really do not want to learn on the job in this case. You should also definitely let someone know of your plans. Tell a trusted friend or family member exactly where you are going and when you plan to be back. Add some time to this estimate as you do not want to worry anyone, only ensure that someone does know to look for you if you do not return. On this note, you may not want to advertise your solo hiking habits too widely. This is especially important for solo women. Unfortunately, the world is not always the safest place and you might not want to broadcast your movements to the world when trekking alone.

Always take your cell phone with you too. Although you may be out of signal range, you will generally be able to find a patch of coverage and this can be a real lifesaver. You should also prepare for an emergency by saving local emergency rescue and police numbers. It can also be really beneficial to leave a trail for people to follow. We're not suggesting breadcrumbs, but rather, park your car in a conspicuous spot and leave the exact details of your chosen trail in an obvious place. Be sure to include the date and estimated times on this as well, as this will allow anyone who finds this information to immediately judge the severity of the circumstances. This can be great in an emergency, as a lone car that is immediately noticeable in a hiking area will ring alarm bells in the local community.

You may also not want to be totally alone, and if you have a dog, they will make a great solo hiking companion. This will add an element of fun to the hike but will also show onlookers that you are not totally alone on the trail. Dogs are also great in the case of a fall where you are unable to move. They will be able to cover some distance around you and make noise that might alert fellow hikers to your presence and circumstances. It is also worth taking something to help you attract attention in such a situation where you do not have the luxury of a canine companion. Reflective gear, flashlights, headlamps, and—as a last resort—flares are a great way of drawing visual attention to a place you may have fallen. A simple whistle is also great in these cases and can be heard for miles around. It might also help, for peace of mind if nothing else, to carry some kind of defensive equipment. Ensure that you remain within the laws when doing so. Hiking poles are a great way to keep animals and people at bay when necessary. Try to find a non-lethal option that gives you a sense of peace of mind. Unfortunately, women do need to be a bit more careful when solo hiking, but with the right preparation, there is nothing to fear.

Most of your fellow hikers will be well intentioned and simply chasing the same experiences you are. They are generally willing to lend a hand, or some advice where necessary and you will very rarely need to worry. The fact is, it is slightly more dangerous to hike by yourself, but by minimizing the risk, you can maximize what you get out of the experience. Many hikers hit the trails to escape their busy everyday lives, and for some, a sense of isolation is a great part of this. Be careful, but do not let yourself be discouraged if you do not have a ready group of hiking enthusiasts in your life.

Permits

Permits vary around the world and it is important that you understand your local legislation and the processes you need to go through. Hiking permits may seem like an irritation, but they play an important role in managing the crowds, particularly in national parks and wilderness areas. As a hiker, you have the responsibility of caring for the trails you take on as well as enjoying them. Hikes that require permits will usually either be very strenuous or in a protected area. They ensure that these trails are not over-walked but also allow you to experience these pristine areas in a more private fashion. Trails that are managed in this way are always far less busy and generally a little further from the beaten track.

So, when do you actually need a permit? Firstly, you will generally need a permit if your trail crosses private land. This simply allows land owners or managers to control the numbers of people passing through. Particularly in rural areas, this can be a very important factor for working farms. You do not want to disrupt someone's work and income. This does, however, also give you the benefit of safety. Such permits indicate to landowners who will pass through and when. This allows them to not only maintain a steady work flow, but also means they will know about your hike and can assist should anything go wrong. Having this added level of safety is vital for hikers on more complex trails and can be a lifesaver. This is generally applied throughout North America, while the rest of the world operates a little differently. In many parts of Europe there is a "right to roam" law that allows hikers designated rights of way or public footpaths which allows hikers to pass over private land in order to access natural features. This does not always encompass camping as well, but there are often designated campsites for hikers. Be sure to research the specific trail you hope to walk and learn about the rules that apply there. In South Africa, there are few trails that pass through private lands or concessions but those that do also generally require a permit.

The importance of a permit in these areas cannot be overstated, as they work to keep you safe. In North America, many parks require both an entry fee and a permit issued for a specific trail in order to carefully monitor the numbers of hikers. Europe is a little different in that many national parks do not require an entry fee and few require hiking permits. Permits are usually only required for overnight hiking and camping. South Africa's national parks have many free trials although many do require permits or entry fees. Generally, there will be an office at the trail base where you can secure a permit right before starting the hike. Many of South Africa's national parks are home to dangerous animals and restrict hiking and walking to guided trails. Many of these parks do not even allow you to exit your vehicle outside of the camps. For your own safety, ensure that you observe these rules carefully wherever you travel.

On lesser known trails, you may need a backcountry permit in North America. These are generally for wilderness areas outside of national parks and private areas. These are also massively important, as these areas can be seriously dangerous. You will generally be further away from society and thus far from help in an emergency. You should never attempt such a trail unless you are absolutely confident in your ability to complete it. When attempting something like this, you should always try to move in groups and secure your permits ahead of time. These will generally be longer trails and will usually involve overnight camping. Extreme trails in North America require a master permit. These are only available to veteran hikers and usually pertain to very challenging and treacherous trails. At this stage of your hiking journey, you shouldn't have to worry about these. In Europe, you only really need to acquire permits for these kinds of long overnight hikes across "backcountry areas." If you are planning to hike in Europe, you should be aware of what is required, but this is a region where permits are not often required. In South Africa, many "backcountry" trails are operated by parks boards or hiking societies. This information should be readily available when researching the trails, and these bodies will generally issue permits for these areas. Try to secure these ahead of time.

The process of acquiring permits is different for almost every individual trail. Some will require that you obtain permits long in advance while others can be obtained on the day of the hike at the base of the trail. We always recommend good preparation and research on these aspects of hiking, so again, try to secure permits as early as possible. This will ensure availability and will allow you to start the trail on arrival rather than lining up at the office beforehand. We will look at trail etiquette in detail further on, but getting the correct permit forms a major part of this. It is really poor form to take on trails without the right permit and can endanger yourself and your fellow hikers. If you are unsure about what permits you require, it is always better to ask someone in the know. National and state parks will always have resources to fill you in as well as a helpline. For more challenging hikes, always consult someone with experience first. Unfortunately, there is no one right answer to the question of permits. Wherever you are, do your own research and get to understand exactly what is required before setting off.

Chapter 4:

What to Do in the Event of an Emergency

You can put as much time and effort into preparation as possible, but emergencies can still happen. Avoiding dangerous situations is not always possible and so it is important to understand what to do if worst comes to worst. Often, emergencies are made worse by poor reactions. Responding quickly and effectively is the best way to address any kind of emergency. Always try to remain calm as you take action. A trail emergency can be incredibly stressful but it benefits no one to overreact. Emergencies range from getting a little lost to injuring yourself to the point of not being able to continue along the trail. This chapter will outline the appropriate responses to likely incidents and should prepare you to calmly and confidently address any kind of scenario.

Assess the Situation

As soon as any kind of disaster befalls you or your party, you need to assess the damage. The most important thing you can do is remain calm. This is a pivotal point and your reaction can make all the difference. If you are alone, you are going to need to keep your head as much as possible and deal with every part of the following. On a guided hike, there will be a leader in charge and you should always take cues from them. However, if you are in an informal group, the first pressing issue is who is going to take charge. Emergency situations necessitate a quick response and decisions cannot be made by committee votes. The most experienced person is always the obvious choice. Give the role to someone you trust to navigate this situation and do it quickly. If you are by yourself, then it is up to you. Now that you are in a place to start responding, you must assess the damage.

What is the actual emergency? You need to decide as quickly as you can, as different scenarios require different actions. Has someone become separated from the group and you are worried that they are lost? Has someone suffered a fall and injured themselves? Are you all lost as a group? These are going to require completely different responses, but once you know what the situation is (no matter what kind), you need to quickly develop a plan. The quicker you respond the better, and so you must decide how best to address the situation. Create a response plan and make sure that everyone in your party is completely clear on their role and the overall objective. For an injury, first aid is going to be the primary focus, while a lost individual is going to need to be searched for. This plan will decide whether the disaster is averted or worsened, so act quickly and confidently.

As the situation develops, you are going to need to monitor everything around you. Are the conditions changing in any way? Are you losing the light? How has the injured person responded to the first aid? Everything is going to be important and you need to be able to adapt the plan if any factors change. During this process everyone in your group should be given a role, even if some people are simply required to watch and help if the need arises. You must also establish whether you need outside help or if this is a situation that the group can adequately handle. If you do need help, then prioritize that and delegate the responsibility to two people. If you are not in signal range, then their job will require moving about searching for connectivity and then making the call. Always err on the side of caution when faced with an emergency. If it is something that may become far more serious, then you should call for help even if it is manageable at the moment.

Lastly, you need to establish whether you are going to be able to move, and if not, someone needs to work on a camp. As a day hiker, you might have to set up something very informal but this is always better than nothing. If there is an injured person among you, ensure they have a sheltered place to lie and wait for help to come. If you are looking for members of your group, then make the shelter as obvious and visible as possible. Light a fire if possible or illuminate the area with headlamps and flashlights. This is good practice whatever the emergency, as rescuers will notice this too. Ideally, you will be prepared with space blankets and whistles to call for attention. Make your camp as obvious as possible and stay in one place unless there is an urgent need to move such as treacherous terrain, the threat of incoming weather, or proximity to a dangerous animal. Also, always stay on or as close to the trail as possible to ensure rescuers know where to look.

Non-Emergency

A non-emergency is an injury or other situation that you can address within the group and will be able to continue on to finish the trail. Essentially, anything that might befall you that can be quickly addressed and moved on from without calling for assistance is a non-emergency. In a situation like this, you will still need to quickly establish what is actually wrong and then take steps to remedy this. The first question you should ask is, "can we realistically move on from this quickly?" With cuts, stings, bruises, minor sprains, and blisters, the answer will generally be "yes." All the hikers in your party should have a first aid kit and this should allow you to quickly address these kinds of issues. Let's take a closer look at these.

Firstly, if someone has fallen and suffered a cut or bruise, what should you do? Always establish severity first. If the cut is bleeding profusely and you are struggling to stem the flow, then you need to call for help immediately. If the bleeding is more manageable though, you should first apply pressure to stop the loss of blood. Once you have stopped the bleeding, you must then disinfect the area. If possible, rinse the wound out with water a little first and then apply disinfectant. Once you have done this, you can apply a plaster, gauze, or a bandage to wrap up the affected area. Once that is completed, reassess the situation and ensure the injured person is able to continue without exacerbating the injury. For bruising, you might apply a cold press if possible, however, these are difficult to keep cool on a hike and so the better option is to simply take pressure off the bruised area as best as possible. Monitor your bruising after arriving home and if you find it does not get better or is getting worse, seek medical attention promptly.

Blisters are a very common hiking injury that you need to deal with effectively to stop them from worsening. We have looked at prevention, but if you do develop blisters on the trail, what should you do? Firstly, you should adjust your shoes and socks if possible. Sometimes loosening your laces slightly will relieve the pressure and stop the blisters being aggravated. Blisters are generally caused by heat, moisture, and excess pressure. When you start a hike, be aware of the feeling in your feet and be particularly wary of any of these. If you notice any hot, wet, or pressured areas, reinforce them with tape or a blister bandage. These will help you to prevent blisters if applied quickly enough, but will also help you mitigate the effects if they have already formed. If you find yourself with full blown blisters, do not burst them. Apply a blister bandage and pad around the epicenter of the problem area to alleviate pressure. If you do have a blister burst on the trail, then treat it as a cut by disinfecting the area and wrapping it up.

Hikers are also susceptible to athlete's foot. A few simple prevention measures will do you very well. Firstly, fungus requires warm, dark, and moist environments to thrive. If you are going to be crossing water regularly on a trail, you need to ensure you are either wearing sandals or breathable shoes and socks that can dry as quickly as possible. It is also a great idea to air out your feet when you stop. Remove your shoes and socks when you stop in order to expose them to sunlight and help your feet and socks to dry out. If you have found that you develop athlete's foot regularly, then consider incorporating more vitamins and antioxidants into your routine. This will boost your immune system and help to prevent athlete's foot. If you do get it, do not worry. Athlete's foot is generally very easily treated. Firstly, you should get an antibacterial soap and antifungal ointment. Wash your feet twice daily with the soap and when completely dry, apply the ointment. During the recovery period, alternate your shoes every day and ensure they are dry. Change your socks regularly and avoid wet public environments such as pools or saunas. You should also avoid scratching the inflamed areas.

Another fairly common trail injury is stings or bites by plants, insects, or animals. Generally, these are fairly easily treatable with ointments or sting/bite cream, but, of course, they can be serious. In serious cases such as snakebites, call for assistance immediately. While many snakes are harmless, unless you are sure of your identification skills, you should call for help as soon as possible. Let's take a look at various problem species among fauna and flora across some great hiking regions. Firstly, in North America there are some plants you should be on the lookout for. Firstly, poison ivy. This is common in the eastern part of North America and has a three leaf formation on its branches. Poison ivy can cause inflammation, rashes, and severe discomfort. Luckily, you can generally deal with this by washing the affected areas. Be careful to wash out your clothes too!

You might also want to keep an eye out for manchineels in the southern parts of North America. The fruits of this tree resemble small apples but are dangerously poisonous and can kill you if consumed. Unless you have experience foraging, never eat anything from a plant while hiking. On a milder note, the plant secretes a white sap that can cause serious swelling and burn-like welts on the skin. Always avoid white sap if you come across it. If you do, however, brush up against this plant, immediately wash yourself thoroughly and remove any trace of the substance. You will still suffer some blistering but this will heal over time. North America is also home to a large variety of snakes. Rattlesnakes are particularly venomous but thankfully they warn people of their presence with their characteristic rattle. Be wary of any snake you find in North America, and in the case of a bite, immediately call for assistance.

Scorpions are also common in much of North America. A good rule of thumb when dealing with these is that they will either have a bigger tail sting or bigger pincers. Scorpions with big stingers are more venomous and usually much more dangerous. Staying away from all scorpions is ideal though. Spiders are also common on hikes. You generally do not need to worry about spiders, although there are some venomous varieties. Check logs and grass patches for spiders before sitting down, as landing on a spider is the surest way of getting bitten. Lastly, bears are fairly common in North America (and rarely in Europe). It may seem counterintuitive, but making noise as you move will discourage bears from approaching, or at the very least, alert them to your presence so that you do not surprise them. If you are face-to-face with a bear, wave your arms—or poles if you have them—above your head and make as much noise as possible. You want to appear large and confident to discourage the bear from attacking. In certain areas, you may even consider carrying bear spray (where this is legal and recommended) as a last resort.

In both Europe and North America, you should watch out for stinging nettles. These have telltale stinging hairs all over their leaves that can cause a stinging rash on the areas where contact has been made. These, too, can generally be washed off to effectively deal with the pain. Generally, this effect does not last longer than a day, and in cases where it does, you should seek medical assistance. Europe is also home to two species of hogweed that are potentially dangerous; the giant and common hogweed. These are weed-like wildflowers with white clusters. The sap of this plant can cause serious blistering when exposed to sunlight and even blindness should it get into your eyes. Again, a thorough wash is your best defense, although you will have to deal with the blistering for a while afterward. It is always wise to avoid any vibrant or fibrous plants wherever possible. Europe is home to fewer snakes compared to the rest of the world, but is still home to several deadly vipers. Again, do not mess around with a snakebite and call for help as soon as possible.

In Europe and the United Kingdom, you are far more likely to encounter livestock than wildlife, and while they often appear harmless, it is best to take care. Sheep and goats do not present much of a threat, although it is best to avoid approaching them as they can be aggressive, even if the actual threat is not that serious. Cattle, on the other hand, should not be messed with on any level. Cows and bulls are deceptive in that they appear mellow, but they are still very heavy animals that can turn on you unpredictably. Bulls should never be approached under any circumstances. If you come to a field with a bull in it, the best advice is to find an alternate route. Never enter that space, as bulls can be savagely dangerous. If you come across a field with cows with their calves and you are with a dog, then extra care needs to be taken, as well as preferably finding an alternative route, because cows can be extremely protective of their young. This is a great idea with animals in general, as there is nothing in the animal world more dangerous than a mother that feels its young is being threatened. If you are not walking with a dog, then you should be able to cross the field without incident, but it is always best to give the cows a wide berth and make sure not to cross between a calf and its mother.

In South Africa, there are several plants to be aware of too. Firstly, euphorbia, which is a large flowering plant that is commonly known as spurges. There are several varieties of these, so looks may differ. However, they also excrete a white sap that can cause irritation to the skin and blindness when in contact with the eyes. Again, avoiding white sap is a great rule of thumb. South Africa is also home to stinging nettles, although less prolifically as the other regions. Here, the same washing method applies. Lastly, South Africa hosts the aptly named pain bush which is a small tree or shrub that produces a creamy sap that causes serious pain along with rashes and blisters. While the pain is intense, the effects should subside after a few days of washing the affected area. In the case of the pain bush, some people are fortunately immune to the effects, although it's best not to test whether you fall into that category. There are a plethora of deadly snakes in South Africa, including the black mamba, one of the world's deadliest, so be particularly careful. If you are bitten by a snake, try to get a photo of it to assist with the treatment, as snake venom varies and knowing which snake bit you can often be a lifesaver. Never approach a snake or attempt to move it. Even the most dangerous snakes are not looking to have a confrontation with you, so the best practice advice here is to simply avoid snakes or give them a very wide berth.

South Africa is home to many dangerous species of animal. From the famous big five (lion, leopard, elephant, rhinoceros, and buffalo), to wild dogs, hyenas, and ostriches, there are many animals that you never want to be near to. Luckily, you will very rarely be able to encounter these animals on foot without a guide accompanying you. There are many more that you might, however. Baboons and monkeys are a constant threat to hikers all around South Africa and will actively attempt to take food off of you. In some parts they will even open cars left unlocked and pillage them of any food. Be very wary of monkeys on the trails, but be especially cautious around baboons. There are also many spiders in South Africa that will bite you if provoked. Many are not actually very dangerous but can cause a spell of nausea, so it's best to avoid spiders wherever possible.

Medical Emergency

If you find yourself in a medical emergency, the most important factor is going to be time. You need to call for assistance as quickly as possible. Wherever you are hiking, you should be prepared with emergency contacts saved in your phone and readily available (see list at the end of this chapter). On a day hike, you will usually be able to find signal range fairly quickly. If you are going to move into multi-day hiking on more treacherous trails, though, it may be worth investing in a satellite phone—but again, day hikers certainly won't need these. The first thing you should tell emergency services is where you are located. You need to give them coordinates that are as specific as possible. Do not think that if you are only attempting short hikes that you needn't pay attention here. We were once on a short four-hour hike where a member of the group ahead of us fell ill to the point of needing evacuation. Be wary that an emergency can happen at any level on any trail.

Coordinates are two sets of numbers that have a degree, a minute reading, and a second reading each. The first coordinate will always be either north or south and the second either east or west. So, where can you find your coordinates? Very simply, if you are within cell phone signal, you can open the compass app (standard on most phones). This will present you with your exact coordinates and you should read these to rescue services and send them to a friend or family member who is not with you. You will also be able to read these coordinates off a map, if you have one, by pinpointing where you are and reading the lines of latitude and longitude. Thankfully, in modern times rescue services are equipped to pick up coordinates as soon as you make contact with them, and it will generally be quicker for them to track you than for you to decipher where you are.

There are a number of other important details that you will need to share with rescue services. It is important that you immediately tell them what has happened and the level of severity of the incident. When telling them this, you should also let them know whether you are equipped to hold your position or not. In peak seasons, rescue lines can become inundated with calls for rescue and they need to know how serious your position is. If you are ill equipped for the situation and in a treacherous position, your rescue will generally be prioritized if at all possible. This is another reminder that it is always better to be prepared for any eventuality. Tell emergency services exactly what kind of injuries people have sustained and how many other people there are in your party too. This is vital information that they will need to facilitate a rescue. Also, be sure to give the rescuers the names of everyone in your group so that they can contact friends and family should this become necessary.

Once you have alerted the relevant authorities, you will need to settle in for a potential night in the wilderness. It is important that you make this bivouac as noticeable as you can. Set up headlamps and flashlights to illuminate the area but always keep one or two as reserves in case of dying batteries. Space blankets are also great reflectors and you should aim your flashlights at them to reflect the light further distances. When spending a night out in an emergency, you should organize a watch overnight so that there are always at least two people alert to movements and sound from rescuers.

Finally, you should also consider starting a fire. When doing this, there are certain important rules to follow. Always clear the area around the fire of any twigs or flammable debris. Starting a forest fire is not going to improve your situation! Stack rocks in a circle to create a semi-sheltered fire pit and ensure that there is always someone tending the fire. Ideally, at least one member of your party will have matches or a lighter, or if you are by yourself, make sure to always carry a lighter and matches in ziplock waterproof bags. If these have been forgotten, do not despair, as a pair of eyeglasses can be used as a magnifying glass to light tinder, although this requires daylight. If night is closing in and you are still without a flame, you are going to need to get a little prehistoric. Gather some tinder with small sticks or husks from plants and place these on top of a bigger stick or branch. Next, find a stick to rub between your hands while pushing it into your base and the tinder. Have your fellow hikers alternate with you as quickly as possible to avoid losing heat and continue until you see an ember among the tinder. Blow on this gently until you catch a flame. Always remember that it is far easier to maintain a fire than it is to start one. If you have a medical emergency by yourself, prioritize calling for help and keeping warm. These will be your two biggest enemies as a solo hiker in an emergency situation.

Emergency Contact numbers:

North America:

- 911 - Emergency Services

- +1-850-283-5955 - Search and Rescue (SAR)

Europe:

- 112 - Emergency Services

United Kingdom:

- 999 - Emergency Services

- +44 (0)20 3817 2006 - Search and Rescue

South Africa:

- 10111 - Emergency Services

- +27 (0)21 937 0300 - Wilderness Search and Rescue

What to Do if You Get Lost

When you realize that you are lost, the first and most important thing you can do is remain calm. There is a simple acronym prescribed by the US Forest Service to remember in this event, "STOP," meaning "stop, think, observe, and plan." So, firstly, stop moving. Take a minute to calm down if you need to and then begin to think. Think about where you have come from and if you passed any memorable landmarks along the way. Check your phone photos to see if there is anything to jog your memory. Take the time you need to think clearly about your situation and try to piece together where you might have gone wrong.

Then, observe what you see around you. Are you on a trail? Have you lost it? What can you see around you and are there any signs of life? In this phase, also consider all the tools at your disposal. If you have a map, phone, compass, or map, then you should use these to the greatest extent possible. Finally, form a plan of action. If you are on a trail, simply backtrack until you find something familiar that will point you in the right direction. If not, try to recall what you should pass as you backtrack. If you are totally lost and unsure of what direction to follow, you might decide to follow a river, stream, or drainage downhill. This should only be an absolute last resort.

Should the situation deteriorate, you may have to spend a night or several in the wild. Again, it is important to stay calm. Follow the steps outlined above and make the best shelter you can. If you are sure of where to go, then continue in the morning. If this is going to be an extended issue, you should consider the following and prioritize them accordingly. Firstly, note how much water you have available. If you are running low, a water source is going to be your first priority. Secondly, you need to regulate your body temperature. Getting too hot or cold in an emergency situation is going to slow you down and can result in sickness and dehydration. Next, address any cuts or scrapes where there is a risk of infection. These may worsen and lead to serious illness, so it's best to keep them clean. Finally, make yourself as noticeable as possible at every stage. Illuminate your camp, wear anything bright or reflective that you have, and light a fire at night. These will give you a much higher chance of being seen and rescued.

As a day hiker, it is unlikely that you will find yourself in these kinds of situations, but it is always better to know what to do. Do not worry unduly about these scenarios, but rather, make a note and be prepared for them if they ever arise. We highly recommend that all hikers take a first aid course. This is a great skill to have generally, but even more so on the trails. Be careful out there and never take unnecessary risks. If you are planning on hiking by yourself, take extra care to prepare for these situations.

Chapter 5:

Weather - Ensuring the Conditions Do Not Ruin the Hike

The weather can ruin many carefully laid plans, but it doesn't have to ruin your hike. With a few extra precautions and a little more preparation, you will be able to hike in any conditions safely. It is important to know how weather can affect a trail so that you can take the necessary measures to go ahead. We have done some of our best hiking in less-than-ideal conditions. Rain and snow can add a level of dynamism and challenge to any hike and so can be very rewarding. It is, of course, important to take extra care. Slippery or icey trails can be a really treacherous path to tread. In this chapter, we will take a look at some ways you can prepare for the weather adequately and ensure you still have a great day outdoors. We'll also look at the effect of the seasons and how best to pick trails all year round.

Know Your Limits

Knowing your limits is always going to help your hike. You need to be sure that you enjoy the outdoors safely and sustainably. If you are just starting out, then avoid hiking in serious weather conditions. If you have planned to try a new trail but have seen the weather forecast and it looks like it will be raining or snowing, do not give up. Rather, adapt your plan to return to a trail you are very familiar with. Rain and snow make trails a lot more unpredictable, although, if you are prepared with decent shoes, this should still be passable. On trails we are quite familiar with, we will generally know where the trail might get a bit slippery or dangerous. On unfamiliar trails, these patches may surprise us and things can end up going terribly. As a beginner, make sure that you are not testing yourself too much all at once. While it is great and important to push ourselves beyond our limits, we have to do so safely. Try to focus on only one aspect of the hike as you take on bigger challenges. For example, focus on distance one weekend and elevation the next, but do not take on both at the same time. Think of the weather as one of these challenges. If there is rain forecasted for your next hike, a familiar trail will prove more challenging and you are still improving. You should also ensure that you have the correct gear and decent shoes if you are braving some inclement weather.

Wind is the silent killer of hiking trails. While snow and rain can be truly menacing, wind is as threatening with the added danger of being constantly underestimated. When checking the weather forecast, always consider wind and then consider your limits in this context. If you are walking into heavy wind, the amount of physical exertion is going to increase and you will need to take that into consideration. Hikers often make the mistake of assuming that wind will be against them one way and with them the other. This is somewhat true, although you will be struggling more throughout because of constant readjustments and strain in your legs. Again, never risk a new hike in heavy winds and stay off of mountains with steep drops. This is also great advice in the case of a lightning storm. It is better not to venture out at all in a violent storm, but if you do, try to stay at as low of an elevation as possible.

While on a hike, you should always be aware of your surroundings, too, and notice how the weather changes. This is an important part of understanding your limits, as you need to realize when the conditions are turning and decide whether to turn back or not. A sudden increase in wind speed along with the darkening of clouds is a sure sign of an approaching thunderstorm. If you are hiking on a mountain, now would be a great time to turn around. If you are on a multi-day hike, then seek shelter. In lowland areas, use your discretion but always be prudent when making these calls. It is important that you always check a forecast before hiking but equally vital that you do not take it as gospel and remain tuned into what is happening around you.

Influence of the Seasons

Seasonal differences on the trails will vary by region quite substantially. As always, be sure to research your specific trail before attempting it and understand the seasonal changes where you live. Anytime of year can be the best time for it, if you are prepared accordingly. Traditionally, spring and autumn are thought of as the best seasons for hiking. Generally, spring and autumn days have milder temperatures without major risk of extreme heat or cold. In colder or higher areas, the snow has usually melted to a great extent and the trails are safer from treacherous footing. In hotter areas, there is less chance of extreme heat and you can usually enjoy a full day on the trails without overheating. We love hiking at these times of year and recommend them to everyone, but especially beginners! This is not a one-size-fits-all rule, though, as the northern parts of North America and Europe can remain snowy and bitingly cold well into these seasons. Inversely, South African hikers can experience extreme heat even during the colder months. Again, always research your particular area.

Summer hiking can be wonderful, too, although you need to be a little wary. We definitely recommend an early start in summer. If you are planning a dawn till dusk hike, arrive at the start of the trail before dawn and set out with the light. Early mornings are far more mild in temperature and are generally clearer in terms of weather. Try to break for lunch at midday and avoid the sun around this time. In lowland areas, the temperatures can be seriously dangerous in the middle of the day. In higher elevations, you may want to prepare with warm clothes even in summer. It is often difficult to gauge temperature or conditions from the base of a trail that has a high elevation gain. Summer is also generally the peak season for animal and tourist activity. Snakes, in particular, become a bigger risk in the warmer months and you should be a little extra cautious. There will also be a lot more people around. This can be aggravating if you are trying to engage with nature, but it also means the trails will be safer. Leaving early is also great for avoiding the crowds. Try to aim for summer days with a bit of a breeze or cloud cover to avoid the most oppressive heat.

Winter may seem a poor choice for hiking, but some of our absolute best hikes have been in the colder months. Assuming you are equipped with warm clothes and sturdy waterproof boots, a winter hike can be truly spectacular. You will generally have a lot fewer people to contend with on the trail, and in higher elevations, and you will be treated to views of snowy vistas. For beginners, try to hike below the snow line in winter, as that is where the real danger begins. In winter, there will also be a lot less animal activity and snakes will mostly be hibernating in colder regions. In lower or warmer climates, a warm winter day can be perfect for avoiding intense heat while still having a very pleasant experience. One thing to note is that when the sun is out in winter, you need to protect yourself. Colder temperatures do not protect you from UV rays, so always take sunscreen. Winter can lull us into a false sense of security with regard to sun protection. Also, always wear a hat.

When we first started hiking, we had a particular trail that we really enjoyed. It was relatively flat with only a small elevation and covered around eight kilometers that we could comfortably pass. The only issue was, we started hiking in summer. When that first winter came, we headed out to the trail, excited to see it in a different seasonal setting. From the moment we started, we knew that this was not at all the trail we knew and loved. The small inclines we used to love were now icy, and we slipped and fell in several spectacularly embarrassing tumbles. By the time we reached the halfway point, we realized that we were walking at just over half the speed of our usual pace. It was seriously grueling and the sun was close to setting by the time we eventually returned to the car. Seasons can severely affect how passable trails are, so always try to know these things before arriving.

Make a Plan and Adapt

Adaptability is going to be a serious asset to any hiker, but particularly when the weather is a major factor. The day before any hike, you should check the weather forecast on a reliable app. There are several very reliable weather apps that you can download for free. Consider the Weather Channel app, AccuWeather, and WeatherBug. These are free apps that work around the world. If you are willing to spend a little money to ensure that you receive accurate forecasts, then also consider Dark Sky or Shadow Weather. These are great apps and are mostly very reliable. The day before setting off will be your first chance to adapt your plan. If the forecast warns of heavy rain, snow, or wind, you may want to alter your route or area altogether. Easier trails will be far better on days with serious conditions. Changing your plans the day before is one thing, but pivoting during a hike is another issue entirely.

While you may have an accurate forecast, there are never any guarantees, and the weather could change unpredictably and quickly. When the weather turns nasty, you need to adapt, and a great starting point is understanding your route. If you know what is ahead of you as well as what is behind you on the trail, then you know immediately whether it is better to keep moving or to turn back. When choosing a trail, make sure to note where the most exposed or treacherous sections are. If you are hiking up a mountain, you will generally be moving into more exposed areas as you progress. If heavy weather blows in on your way up, it will generally be better to turn back, as it will get worse as you continue. For circular trails through forests or lowlands, this will vary a lot more. Trails can lead you through a changing landscape with different terrains. Knowing what lies ahead is going to be a huge asset when thinking about your options.

Sometimes your best option is to simply give it some time. If you are in a sheltered spot when the rain or snow comes down, perhaps stay put for a few minutes. This will allow you to avoid the worst of the precipitation and will give you time to formulate a plan. Treat this break as any other and try not to stay put for too long. Eat something, have a drink of water, and then execute your plan. If you do plan on a day hike in less-than-ideal conditions, you may want to consider some items you can use for shelter. An umbrella should be adequate for rain and snow on a day hike, but if you are venturing onto longer trails, then perhaps consider a more solid shelter like a small lightweight tent, a tarpaulin, or a space blanket. Try to avoid getting too wet, as this is going to slow you down and make everything a little more challenging.

Read the signs around you as you are walking and take note of sudden changes. A quick pickup in the wind may indicate a pressure system passing through. This is essentially either a patch of higher or lower air density to what surrounds it and often indicates an oncoming storm. A steady increase in wind speeds could also indicate that a storm is coming, as well as more obvious signs such as clouds gathering and darkening. If you are in an exposed area and need to take shelter but have not brought any protection with you, you have several options. If you are in a lowland area, try to find a patch of coverage that is slightly elevated. Water is going to pool and potentially even flood at the lowest level. Avoid these areas to stay as dry as possible. In heavy winds, shelter is a little more obvious. Find an area of flatground with trees, shrub, or rock formations between you and the wind. If you are hiking up a mountain and the wind picks up to a great extent, it is generally safer to turn back, especially because the higher you get the worse the wind will feel and the less likely you will be to find shelter.

If you are hiking up a mountain and rain starts to fall, avoid steeper areas and look for sturdy outcrops above you for some cover. If you are in higher elevations and a lightning storm comes through, then you should seek cover as low as possible. Lightning strikes are far more common higher up and so you should attempt to distance yourself from any highpoints, including tall trees that might seem like good shelter. When in the midst of an electrical storm, you will be able to judge the distance of lightning with a simple counting method. Once you see the flash of lightning, count the seconds that pass until you hear thunder. Divide the total by five and you will have the distance in miles. So, if five seconds passed, the lighting struck a mile away. A mile is equivalent to 1.6 km. If the strike is within a mile, you should consider turning back and heading indoors. When this is not an option, try to get low to the ground by crouching but do not lie flat, as this puts you at risk in the case of a nearby ground strike. If you are on an exposed high point, move off of it as quickly as possible. Never shelter under a single tree, but seek coverage in wooded areas if possible. Lastly, stay out of water or wet areas and avoid anything that may conduct electricity such as steel fences, train tracks, and powerlines entirely. Once the lightning starts to strike, take cover and monitor the situation. If the storm is moving away from you, then it is generally safe to continue. If the lightning keeps coming closer, you may want to head for home if it is safe to move off.

A recent study published by National Geographic shows that injuries and weather are the two biggest causes of emergency situations among hikers, and so conditions should not be underestimated. This study also shows that day hikers are often more susceptible to poor situations turning dangerous because they are generally less prepared in terms of what they are carrying. If you are considering a hike in inclement weather, you may want to carry some extras just in case. Some extra food and water as well as some warm clothes and potentially a shelter of some kind will set you up for any emergency situations. Rescuers are unlikely to begin a search, as the light is fading or there is heavy weather, so being prepared for a night on the trail is really important when the weather is a concern. Standard practice in most search and rescue operations is to begin at first light.

Walking through rain or snow is also going to increase your risk of getting lost. Trails become a lot harder to discern when covered with snow or rained out. National Geographic reports that of 100 rescue missions in a year at Great Smoky Mountains National Park in the United States, 90% of the rescues were of day-hikers with the majority becoming lost due to an injury or weather. If you are confronted with heavier weather than you expect and feel even a little unprepared to tackle the challenge, it's best to turn back. There is no sense in putting yourself at risk to complete a hike, especially in poor conditions. Rescues also become far more challenging in adverse conditions, and if you do find yourself in an emergency situation, you will be far harder to find.

So, what do you do if the weather seems to be changing for the worse on the trail? The most important point is to monitor the situation. Give yourself a measure, and if the conditions deteriorate, then turn back. If you are around the half-way point on a circular trail, you need to know what is ahead of you. If rain, wind, or snow picks up at this point, you must decide fairly quickly whether it is safer to continue or turn around. It may be tempting to simply continue from this point, but turning back gives you the advantage of having seen the trail already, and so minimizes your chances of becoming lost. Unless you are sure the terrain ahead is more protective, backtracking is the more desirable option. If you are on a trail network and have the option to change trails to head back more directly, this may be an attractive option. Again, prior preparation will make this an easier decision. If you are not sure of the route, then backtrack. If you do, however, know that a change of trail can get you back to safety quickly, then opt for that route. With weather, it is always better to err on the side of caution. If the conditions turn on you, turn around and head for home. Even confident and experienced hikers can be put out by weather, so whatever your level, prioritize safety.

Chapter 6:

Food and Water

Food and water are your fuel on a hike and so should be carefully considered. Many hikers make the mistake of taking too little or too much food and water. Both can place an unnecessary burden on your body. In this chapter, we will explore ways that you can ensure you have all the sustenance necessary to finish a hike feeling good. A lack of quality nourishment can result in injury or even prolonged illness, so it is important to take note. We will look at the right foods for a hike too. It will slow you down to carry a lot of food that is not serving you the way it should. Think about the amount of energy you require for a hike and prioritize lightweight power foods that give you the most out of a little. As highlighted in the previous chapter, it is important to take extra food in case of an emergency, however, this is not the same as overloading yourself with snacks. Plan ahead carefully and always be aware of what you are carrying and the rates at which you consume them.

Nutrition

Taking the wrong food on a hike can be an absolute nightmare. You want to fuel your body effectively without risking any kind of upset. Let's start at the beginning. Eating before a hike is an often overlooked aspect of hiking nutrition. An ideal breakfast on the day of a hike will include and focus on complex carbohydrates and lean proteins. This can include a wholewheat sandwich with peanut butter, as well as things like bananas, eggs, yogurt and berries, porridge, or nuts and raisins. Carbohydrates are a very effective pre-hike meal that will allow you to maintain a good level of energy on the trails while proteins will ensure healthy muscles and bones. Starting off the right way can make a huge difference to the way you feel on the trails, and the better you feel, the easier it will be to complete.

Next, you will want to pack for the day's adventure. Non-perishable and lightweight foods are best for a hike. Packing sandwiches may seem like a great idea, but if you are hiking in the heat, they may be a little funky by the time you hit lunch. In cold weather hiking, this is more reasonable. Trail mix is an absolute classic as far as hiking snacks go. A mixture of dried fruit and nuts is going to give you great energy reserves and are super easy to carry. Nuts and dried fruits individually are equally great. You may also look for some snack bars for the trail, like protein bars or granola clusters. These are also effective sources of energy and can be easily consumed on the move. A pasta salad is also a healthy fuel and is less susceptible to heat than bread or sandwiches. Nutritionists recommend between 65g and 75g of dry pasta. This is a good benchmark for getting the right amount of carbohydrates and you can usually get to approximately this amount by filling both hands when cupped. Otherwise, leave the pasta out of the salad and take some tortillas to combine instead and you will have a real feast. Dried meats such as beef jerky in North America and biltong in South Africa are a great source of protein and are easily carried. When packing for a trek, try to avoid sugary foods. These will give you a burst of energy but won't sustain you very much. Sugar will also dehydrate you faster. If you need a sweet treat, take fruit instead, as this natural source of sugar is far more beneficial.

After a hike, you will need to replace all the nutrients spent that day. Try to eat as soon as you can after arriving home and ensure that once again you focus on proteins and carbohydrates. Lean meats like chicken and fish, including tuna, salmon, and mackerel, are great for replenishing the body, and paired with some wholewheat bread or pasta, they make a great post-hike dinner. For vegetarians, chickpeas, red kidney beans, and butter beans are a great source of protein. Cheese might be good for after a hike, but avoid it beforehand, as it will take a long time to digest and give you a heavy feeling for the duration of the day. Mix in a healthy dose of vegetables and you will feel amazing come morning. Eating after a hike is important because your body will be looking to reenergize and recover. This is another vital aspect of hiking nutrition that is often overlooked.

So, now that you're out on the trail, how often should you actually consume what you have brought? We recommend eating at least every two hours to ensure that you have the required energy. Do not gorge yourself at every stop, but rather snack constantly throughout the day. Eating small amounts regularly is going to allow your body to metabolize the food faster and will keep you light on your feet. You do not want to eat a heavy meal on a hike, as this is going to make you feel a bit lazier and will leave your stomach feeling shaky. Carbohydrates are great for giving you energy but try to balance them out with proteins and fruits to avoid feeling bloated as you walk. Carbohydrates also absorb water and too many might lead to running out of water faster. Carbohydrates are broken down into sugars that enter the bloodstream, and this is what gives you energy. Too many carbohydrates can lead to increased blood sugar levels that might haze your level of concentration or result in an energy crash as they are absorbed. Carbohydrates are good for hiking but make sure to balance them with other foods.

Lastly, let's look at some foods to avoid. Greasy, fatty, and deep fried foods are ones to avoid before and during a hike. Our bodies convert fats to energy far less efficiently, with the result being that you feel heavier and may crash at some point. As mentioned, cheese, and also milk, is metabolized slowly and often leaves you feeling bloated and heavy. This is certainly not ideal for hiking, so try to avoid cheeses as much as possible before and during a hike. Chocolates and candy are also really poor options that are going to spike your energy levels right before an inevitable crash. This is going to leave you sleepy and unmotivated. It is best to stick to health bars and fruits. The same goes for sodas and fizzy beverages; these will also actually dehydrate you as you walk. Stick to water to be safe. Spices are also to be avoided pre-hike. Spices are great for flavor but often disrupt the stomach and intestines, leading to indigestion and heartburn, and will leave you feeling sluggish on the trail. Finally, do not make the mistake of drinking fruit juice before a hike. While fruit is a great source of energy, most juices are laden with excess sugar that is going to dehydrate you and lead to a dip in energy levels.

Hydration

Water is going to be your best friend on a hike. If you ensure a constant intake of water, you will feel better and be able to move more effectively. Water is, however, fairly heavy, and you do not want to weigh yourself down too much on the trails. Firstly, drink around four glasses of water before setting out. This will start you off well and just means that you have less to carry on your back. A good rule of thumb is to pack one liter of water for every two hours of hiking. This is also a great measure of how quickly you should be consuming water. Always remember to pack a little extra so you have some margin for error. You should also account for two main factors: temperature and terrain. Over tougher terrain you will expend more energy, and so you should take more water. The same applies to temperature. If you are walking on a hot day, then take extra care and pack more water for the trek. On colder days, try to stick to the above ratio.

If you are a prolific coffee drinker, you may be wondering about how this can affect your energy levels on a hike. Rest assured that there are some benefits, however, it is also good to know about potential side effects. A morning coffee before a hike is going to energize you and help you to stay focused. This is great for early mornings where you may be lacking a little motivation. Caffeine is also great for endurance in that it ensures your body retains glucose and relies on fat storage as you exert energy. This is great, as you will be able to keep moving and give your body a better workout overall. Coffee beans also contain many healthy antioxidants and nutrients. If you are a veteran coffee drinker, have that cup before heading out. That being said, there are some downsides. Firstly, coffee is a natural diuretic, meaning you may have to stop for a few extra pee breaks. You may also develop an upset stomach as you march the trails and this will slow you down. If you are not traditionally a coffee drinker, then perhaps it's best to avoid it, but otherwise the benefits may surpass the downsides.

Now that you are energized and hydrated and raring to go, how should you carry water? There are two main options here; the classic water bottle, or a hydration pack or bladder. This is going to vary person-to-person but may be worth considering some aspects of the debate.

Water bottles are less likely to spill. Soaking your supplies is a sure recipe for a bad mood on a hike and can prevent you from being able to warm up if this is required. Bottles are also easier in terms of filling and pouring. If you are on a trail that offers fountains or a water source, then a bottle is easiest. If you are going to share water or make tea (for example), a bottle is the clear winner. However, a bladder allows you to drink freely on the move and is generally lighter and less bulky to carry. If you are trying to move quickly without many stops, then a bladder may be better for you. Bladders also generally have a much larger capacity than water bottles. They are, however, a little deceptive in that you cannot easily judge how much you have consumed. This may throw you off a little if you run out early. Bladders also inevitably form a leak after extended use and need to be replaced fairly frequently, so consider your options.

Lastly, in terms of drinks to absolutely avoid on a hike, the list is short but important. Never drink untreated water or from unfamiliar streams, rivers, and dams. This will often upset the gut and be very poor for your walking form. Even mountain streams risk contamination, so always be cautious. You should also avoid alcohol. This will dehydrate you quickly and also impair your coordination and focus. It's best to leave the cold beers in the fridge for afterward. Dairy products like milk and drinking yogurt are also not ideal on the trails. These may make you feel very heavy and can also upset the stomach. Finally, avoid carbonated beverages, especially sugary ones. We have looked at the effect of sugar, but more generally these will make you gassy and could lead to discomfort as you walk. Try to stick to good old-fashioned water when hiking, as well as exercising, and you should be good to go.

Early in our hiking journey we were heading out to a trail first thing in the morning. We had both had a very intense and demanding week leading up to the day. We were feeling rather tired, and so we stopped and got two energy drinks. We thought they would be perfect for keeping us awake and starting the day off right. The sun was just emerging fully from behind the horizon and we set off feeling very energized indeed. Almost three hours into a seven, or so, hour hike, we just crashed. We were like zombies trudging up that trail and seemed to lose energy with every step. We had to stop so often on that trail, and one of us even fell asleep at one point. It was simply not worth it. Drink coffee if you wish, but otherwise just stick to water!

Chapter 7:

Navigation

Getting lost is one of the more dangerous risks involved in hiking, and so it is best to avoid it at all costs. The best way to avoid this is to stick to the trails and plot out your route ahead of time. In this chapter, we will look at some helpful navigation techniques that will prevent the risk of getting lost. In our modern age, we have a plethora of options available to us that make navigation a simpler task. Nothing beats the classics, however, and an understanding of map reading and the use of a compass may come in handy when all else fails. Always be prepared ahead of time and understand the terrain and direction you will be taking. As always, you would rather not get lost at all, but these skills will help you should the time ever come.

Getting Around

While maps may seem archaic when your mobile phone can easily navigate you from A to B, hiking is often going to lead you out of signal range. Being able to read a map and having one on hand is always a great idea. There are many different types of maps, and knowing which ones to use for different purposes is the best start to becoming a successful navigator. If you used to have a globe in your geography class, you're probably already familiar with a physical map. A physical map is one that shows features of different landmasses and nations. For example, mountain ranges, deserts, forests, and rivers are all shown on physical maps. You may be interested in having a look at one in the general vicinity of your desired hike, but generally these are not the best fit for our purposes. Political maps are those that show us nation states and their borders. These will show country names and capital cities and occasionally states or provinces. Again, perhaps interesting to look at, but not the ideal hiking asset.

As a hiker, you will generally want to use a topographical map. Colloquially known as topo maps, these show physical features of a landscape as well as contour lines. These demarcate areas of an equivalent height above sea level. Contour lines are very important for hikers and show elevation. This allows us to see where trails rise and fall, as well as where to expect valleys, ravines, and cliffs. This is a very useful tool to have and be able to read. Where contour lines are close together, this indicates a steeper slope, while contour lines spaced far apart indicate a gentle rise. You will generally find that every fifth line is bold, and this is known as a reference line. Each map will have a scale which allows you to tell the height each line shows. Generally, the lines occur at around 10 meter intervals, but be sure to check your specific map. Topographical maps also have the benefit of being very detailed in terms of their symbols. There will generally be a key on these maps with symbols that show certain things and places such as camping areas, fishing spots, food services, hiking trails, and emergency services offices. Topographical maps walk the line between detail and easy reading. Having said that, they do take some getting used to.

Do not simply buy a map book and head out without having opened it first. Although topo maps are fairly straightforward, you do not want to be working this out when you are already on the trail. Take some time to familiarize yourself with the area prior to setting out. Mark any points of interest you may see, such as parts of the trail with steep inclines or prominent landmarks, or features such as lakes. This is a great way to get a sense of what the trail is going to look like and how long it may take to pass. It will also highlight any challenging sections and note any alternative routes for emergencies. You should also note where you will find any water sources and plan accordingly with your supplies. Before setting out, you should practice using the scale, and once on the trail, make an effort to visualize what you have worked out previously. If you are able to translate the scale on the page into the world around you, you will have a far better idea of the trail, the distances involved, and the level of elevation you will deal with.

Topographical maps are available fairly widely in a digital format now as well. Downloadable (so they work without signal) and interactive maps are available for many national parks and hiking areas around the world, and you might want to look into this if visiting a new area or trying unfamiliar trails. While on the subject of digital navigation, let's think about GPS systems, how to use them, and the different types of navigation systems. Firstly, differential GPS systems are those found in smart phones. This is a system whereby data from ground stations is measured against satellite positions to pinpoint your location, and this data can be layered over a map. This is a very accurate navigation system, although they are dependent on signals and so can be interrupted by buildings and tall trees. The mapping apps on your phone use this type of navigation system. Non-differential GPS systems work directly through satellites and so are less accurate than their alternative. They do, however, have a far broader range and are much more practical in remote areas.

Another important distinction to make is the difference between mapping and non-mapping GPS systems. Our mobile phones use mapping GPS systems, and this layers our position and destination over a map and can give us specific instructions to get there. A GPS like this may tell you to "turn right now." Non-mapping GPS systems can give you coordinates of your location and can point you in the correct direction if you have inputted another coordinate. It has a limited visual display and will not show you trails or obstacles along the way. Most differential GPS systems work with a programmed map and some non-differential systems do as well. A non-mapping GPS system and a topographical map of your area are a perfect combination. You will be able to locate yourself on the map very easily and know which direction to take while also being able to identify features and trails along the way. This is a better pairing than a topo map and a mapping GPS, as these two might conflict and contradict each other. Either use a mapping GPS that you are confident in or use a non-mapping GPS to show you where you are on your topo map.

If you do not want a GPS system and would rather have something a little more traditional, a compass is the perfect tool. If you can read a topo map effectively and are able to note directions with a compass, you will be able to find your way with no problem. If you want to navigate like this, it is very important that you know how to use a compass as well as the type you will need. A compass has four main parts. Firstly, the baseplate, which is the bottom part of the compass and usually has at least one straight edge marked with a ruler to work out scale on a map and line up the map and compass correctly. Next, there is a direction of travel arrow, generally at the top of the compass. This is also used for map orientation. You will find a circular piece in the middle known as the rotating bezel. This piece is adjustable, yet inside there is a magnetic needle which you cannot adjust yourself. At the most basic level of explanation, using a compass is fairly straightforward. Assuming you have a topographical map, you will line up the direction of the travel arrow with the top of the map with a straight edge keeping it in line with the map on one side. Next, adjust the bezel to match the compass on the map. Finally, turn your body in a circle with the map and compass held flat until the direction of travel or direction on the map lines up with the magnetic needle. If you are going to use this method, you should practice this technique thoroughly before trying it on the trail.

There are three main types of compass that you should be aware of before buying one for yourself: a baseplate compass, a mirrored baseplate compass, and a lensatic compass. A baseplate compass is the most simple, and as a beginner hiker, this is a great option. These are also usually transparent for easily seeing the map below. It can, however, only really be used for finding a bearing or direction. Mirrored baseplate compasses, on the other hand, have a little more functionality. They are also called sighting compasses and can be used to measure the height of a slope as well as its angle. This can be great if you are going to venture into more challenging multi-day hiking. Lastly, the lensatic compass is the most advanced and is used widely by soldiers and military personnel. It works similarly to a mirrored baseplate compass and has the same functionality with a slightly different method of doing so. They also fold out and one edge can be used as a ruler as well as containing other mapwork tools. For starters, we recommend a simple baseplate compass. This should meet the needs of a beginner and intermediate hiker perfectly.

Are You Allowed to Be Here?

Another really important aspect of understanding where you are going is knowing where you are not permitted to go. It is not always so obvious as a barbed wire fence with a sign that reads "keep out!" So, let's have a look at how to make sure you are not trespassing. You need to know where you are and are not allowed to be. This is very important. Never ever climb a fence to access an area, even if you believe a trail leads that way. This is very poor form and may result in some trouble with landowners. Studying a map of the trail beforehand will help you to identify any potential areas to avoid and you should bear these in mind as you go. If an established trail does cross private land, you will generally be able to do so with an obvious entry and exit point. There may be a gate or stile and you should use the designated points to move through. If you are unsure about certain areas, it is perhaps best to avoid them or move around. Certain landowners will require you to get a permit or let them know that you will be crossing. Where this is the case, always comply. Researching a trail beforehand is a great way to find out about any potential pitfalls or administrative requirements that you should meet beforehand.

When researching the trails, you should also be on the lookout for features. Topo maps are a great resource for seeing if any areas along the trail are going to be prohibited or impassable, but also let you identify any points of interest along the way. Mapping GPS systems also allow this and will even highlight no-go areas. Online resources will also generally draw your attention to any impassable or out-of-bounds areas along the trail and you should take careful note of where these are. Whenever you are researching a hike, you should look out for anything that catches your interest. Topo maps are great for gaining an idea of the landscape, as you will be able to see slopes and high points and identify any potential stopping points with a great view. You might also defer to someone with a little more expertise or experience. If you know any hikers who have completed trails on your to-do list, ask them all about the areas and what features you should visit, as well as if any areas are closed off to the public. You could also phone park offices or concessions where there are hiking trails and ask the staff about the different trails and anything that you should consider.

Chapter 8:

Etiquette

Good form and etiquette is an important but overlooked aspect of hiking and you should take note of the following suggestions as you venture out onto the trail. This chapter is going to dive into considerations for other hikers and how to hike sustainably and leave no trace. We are hikers because we love nature and we have to show it the respect it is due. There is nothing more frustrating than litter or signs of human activity on trails or in campsites and so we urge you to take care of the areas around you as you enjoy the sights and sounds of nature. This goes beyond simple aesthetics as the traces we leave behind can have a profound impact on the fauna and flora that call it home. You should always leave a place as you found it if not in a better state.

The Countryside Code

We cannot simply blaze trails wherever and whenever we want. Instead, there is the countryside code. This is a list of suggestions to ensure that you enjoy any activity in the countryside safely and sustainably. The code exists to keep residents and visitors to the country in a harmonious relationship rather than an acrimonious one, both with each other and with the land. The first point relates closely to this, respecting people who live or work in the country. Be courteous and friendly to the people you encounter and do not disrupt their activity in any way. Next, you should be aware of where you are allowed to go and who has the right of way. As discussed in the previous chapter, these are really important factors and you should always be aware of them when out in nature.

Next, you should be aware of any land that is being cultivated and avoid treading on it. If you can see that land has been plowed or that plants are being grown there, walk around. You don't realize the effect that walking through such an area can have and you need to be very careful not to disrupt any farming activities. This is the same for domestic animals and wildlife. Do not disrupt them or interact with them at all if it can be avoided. Sometimes animals will approach you out in nature or as you walk through farmland and there is not much you can do. However, you should never approach animals. It may be tempting, especially with domestic animals, but you never know how they will react or how it will affect their temperament. Simply let animals be, no matter where you encounter them.

You should also always use the designated trails, gates, and paths and leave all of these as you found them. You will usually encounter closed gates. If they are closed when you arrive, let yourself through and then close them behind you. Leave no litter on the trails and do not disrupt the paths in any way. Also, never interfere with any buildings or machinery that you may find as you progress. As you walk, be sure to collect all of the litter you generate and carry it home with you to dispose of properly. You should also not make excessive noise as you walk. This all really boils down to respecting the people and places around you in the country. You must also take care not to leave a fire unattended or create any potential fire hazards. It is also generally recommended that if you come across a small fire that is unattended in the country, you either put it out immediately or report it to someone who will.

If you are trekking with a dog, you need to keep it under control according to the countryside code. If your dog is not very well trained to walk alongside you, then be sure to keep them on a leash at all times. While it may be tempting to let your pooch run around wildly and enjoy the surroundings, you need to ensure they are not having a negative impact on the environment around them. Please take care both for your own safety and for that of your dog. Be honest with yourself about your canine companion's level of training. If there is any doubt about whether they will run off or hassle wild or domestic animals, then keep it on a leash at all times. You should also be aware that in the country, you will often have to pass through gates and over stiles. If you have chosen a route with many such obstacles, think carefully about whether it is practical to take your dog. While it is incredibly rewarding to trek with a dog, you need to ensure their safety, your own, and minimize their impact wherever possible.

Right of way is an important concept on hiking trails as it keeps people safe and prevents dangerous situations. The only places where these may not apply are where you see specific signage that outlines a different policy or different rules. Firstly, if you are coming down a hill or a slope, you need to yield to those coming up. People ascending a trail have the right of way because it is far easier to regain momentum on the way down. Climbing up is a lot more physically taxing and so you should let these hikers pass.

If you are hiking in an area that allows mountain biking as well and the trails mix somewhat, know that you, as a hiker, have the right of way. Cyclists should yield to you and let you pass. Unfortunately, however, these fellow adventurers may not be sure of these guidelines, so it is always better to be vigilant and not simply assume that they are going to stop. It is their responsibility to be as familiar with these principles as you, however, that is not always a reality. Again, it is far easier for a cyclist to regain momentum than it is for a hiker. Where this rule is not observed, do not fly off the handle, rather, simply let the cyclist know that in the future they should yield. Where hiking trails mix with horse riders, you as the hiker should yield and let the animal through. This applies to any kind of ridden or pack animal such as donkeys, camels, cattle, and oxen. This is for your safety as well as the animals. It can be very difficult to halt pack animals, particularly if there are a group of them, so keep an eye out and move aside for them.

If you are wanting to overtake a hiker in front of you on the trail, you are well within your rights to do so. Try to approach politely and make yourself known rather than just barging through. You might say "excuse me" or "thank you" as you pass, and always offer a greeting as well. This is good practice on the hiking trails and doing so in a friendly way is going to help keep hiking a friendly and social activity. If you are moving faster than those in front of you, you do have the right of way, but always try to be graceful about this.

These cover most of the etiquette guidelines around the world, however, you should research your specific region and see if there are any differences that you should note. You may want to note that in South Africa, the countryside code stipulates that you should never walk alone if this can at all be avoided. This region can be a little unsafe and you do not want to put yourself in harm's way. In North America, some hiking trails overlap with hunting areas. In these areas, you need to wear orange or yellow so that you are immediately separable from wild animals. This can really be a life or death decision, so understand where you are going and the implications of that area.

Bathroom Breaks

If you are on a dawn to dusk hike, then odds are you are going to need the restroom at least once. This may be awkward at first, but don't worry, you will get used to it. There are some factors to bear in mind, however, when you do the deed. Before setting out at all, you need to research the specific trail you are on or the nature reserve you are in. Many places have certain rules about where and how to conduct the transaction between body and earth. Generally speaking, the following will apply. Firstly, move off the path and find somewhere quiet. It will be equally horrible for you and another person if they come into view when you are midway through taking care of business. Ensure you find a secluded spot that offers a lot of protection and is unlikely to be stumbled upon. Be aware of what is around you and stay at least 70 paces (but ideally more) from anywhere occupied by humans or water sources.

Next, you should leave absolutely no trace above ground. Take a camping trowel and dig a hole at least 15 cm deep. This hole will be your toilet. Again, your research will come into play here. Many parks and trails require that you do not bury toilet paper in the ground. This is generally good practice anyway. So, you have two options here, either take a ziplock bag where you can stash the used toilet paper until you can dispose of it properly, or use leaves. Please take care to only use leaves that you know are harmless. Using a bushel of poison ivy or stinging nettles for this purpose is going to scar you physically and emotionally for years to come. While leaves may be slightly uncomfortable depending on the surrounding foliage, at least you won't have to carry anything out with you. Once you've wrapped up, cover the hole with the same soil you removed and place an upright stick in the place to prevent fellow hikers from digging in the same area. We recommend always taking some hand sanitizer or waterless soap to keep this process as hygienic as possible. Urinating is often a lot more simple and discreet. You should, however, never go anywhere near a water source or campsite. Again, the 70 paces rule applies. In large bodies of water or where you are downstream from human activity, you should be alright just "taking a swim." Always be considerate and think about how you are affecting fellow hikers.

Potential Penalties

While there are possible consequences for breaking the countryside code around the world or when addressing the call of nature incorrectly, fear of punishment should not be your main motivator. The world's natural spaces are such a profound resource that feeds our souls and allows us to have wonderful hobbies like hiking, mountain climbing, and trail running. You should respect natural places for no other reason than gratitude for what you have gained from them. That being said, in North America, littering is illegal and leaving behind residue on hiking trails can lead to fines or even community service. In the UK, you will also receive a fine for littering of up to £150, or €100 in mainland Europe. South Africa carries serious penalties for littering and dumping, including potential jail time, although these are rarely enforced.

If you ignore the countryside code and cross land by climbing fences and trekking through fields, pastures, or paddocks, you may run the risk of having a charge of trespassing against you. This can be very serious. In North America, trespassing can result in up to a $5000 fine in the United States and up to $10,000 in Canada, with similar penalties in Europe. In the UK, you may face jail time of up to 51 weeks in prison or heavy fines. If you are caught trespassing in South Africa, you may face the harsh punishment of two years in prison. It's best not to risk it at all. Finally, if you are caught incorrectly using the bathroom outdoors, penalties may apply, although you will generally just get a rebuke and a severely embarrassing situation. Similar fines to littering may apply, however.

Personal and Environmental Health

Beyond legal implications, a lack of respect for the wilderness may have many other consequences. We have prioritized keeping you safe throughout this book and this is really the core value of the countryside code. In terms of respecting the people in the countryside, there may not be a direct threat to your personal health, but remember that in many places, the locals are going to be keeping an eye out and responding to emergencies that may occur. Maintaining a good rapport with the people around you is going to allow them to do so without hesitation, not only for you personally but for fellow hikers and outdoor explorers in future. Respecting the animals in an area is going to have a much more direct impact should you fail to comply. Wild animals are going to be unpredictable. Even experts often have unfortunate encounters, so do not push your luck ever. Do not approach the wildlife and show them due respect at all times. Remember that this is their domain and you are simply a guest. Treat them accordingly at all times.

The same applies for domestic animals. You can never really understand the implications of entering a field with cows, sheep, or goats. While they may appear more friendly and approachable than wild animals, they, too, can be unpredictable. Interacting with these animals can also have a severe impact on the animals' health. Stress is not only a human quality—it can have real consequences for animals too. Dairy cows are known to yield less milk if they are stressed, and in sheep and female cows, stress can affect a pregnancy negatively. Beyond the implications for the animals themselves, you do not want to have a negative impact on commercial activities in areas that you visit. This may make the farmers less inclined to allow wandering through their property. This applies also to closing gates and ignoring machines as you trek. Leaving a gate open that is meant to contain farm animals is going to seriously disrupt farming and you do not want this on your conscience.

If you choose to ignore paths and beat your own trail through wild or farming lands, you are also going to put yourself at risk. You will be far more difficult to locate should an emergency befall you and you may affect vegetation negatively. Particularly in national parks and farmlands, the paths are specifically laid out to minimize human impact on local flora and crops. That leads us to environmental impact. The countryside code has been developed to prevent negative environmental conditions such as forest fires and amounts of litter. If you are leaving trash in your wake as you hike, then your impact can be very negative on the trails and environments you traverse. A fire can be truly devastating on an ecosystem and so you should take extra care any time you are starting a campfire. The only difference between a wildfire and a campfire is control, and once it is lost, it is seriously challenging to regain. Never start a fire unless you are sure you are in an area where it is permitted and you know how to keep it under careful control.

Finally, never leave anything behind. When clearing a campsite, be sure to double-check the surroundings. This also applies to areas that you have used as a restroom. Leave no trace and please never bury any trash with your waste. You do not want to negatively impact the health of the soil by introducing foreign objects. Never pick any flowers or plants to take with you, either, as this can be detrimental to the environment. In a field of wildflowers this may be very tempting, but it is always better to simply enjoy the view and let the plantlife be. We are not trying to scare you with any of these consequences, rather, we simply want to stress the importance of respecting the areas around you.

Chapter 9:

Hiking With Children and Pets

Hiking can be an incredibly beneficial activity for children, as it helps them to live an active lifestyle while also stimulating an interest and respect for the natural world. Dogs also benefit and can offer great companionship on the trails. In this chapter, we will take a look at some things to consider when taking your child or pet out into nature. Always prioritize respect and ensure that you teach your children the importance of maintaining a healthy and mutually beneficial relationship with the outdoors. You should also consider safety very carefully and make a concerted effort to keep yourself and your companions out of harm's way. Let's take a look.

Children

Getting your kids interested in nature is one of the most rewarding things you can ever do. This will give your kids a wonderful opportunity to be active and interested in the world around them. A few slight adjustments to your itinerary and the gear you pack will ensure your children are safe and stimulated as they trek alongside you. Firstly, make sure that your first aid kit caters to them as well. Have a few smaller bandages and Band-Aids on hand in case of any mishaps. Also be careful to take any specialized medications your child may need such as an asthma pump or epipen, if they are allergic to bees. You should also equip your children with the right gear. Make sure they have good footwear, a hat, a water bottle, and a jacket. It is as important for your children to have adequate gear, as it is for you, and you should not overlook this. If you have young children, you may want to get a carrier pack, as well, in case they cannot walk for stretches of the trail. These can be a lifesaver for an exhausted child, although you need to make sure that you have a good one. Practice carrying your child in the pack at home and test whether it puts any additional pressure on your back. If it does, try to adjust it to sit more comfortably. If the issue persists, maybe find one that is a little better structured.

You are going to need to select trails that are rather short and try to choose ones with features your children will enjoy. Children are surprisingly able to cover reasonable distances, but do not go for something too challenging in the beginning. You should also let your children set the pace because if they are racing to keep up, they are going to expend way more energy and tire out much quicker. Think about your child's age and level of fitness before selecting a hike. You should also be very careful to ensure your kids are drinking enough water, eating well before and on the trail, and are adequately protected from the sun. Take ample sunscreen to apply to your children as often as is required. Allow them to carry their own water but encourage them to take drinks when you do to ensure they are hydrated as you walk. In terms of food, give your children the same type of protein and carbohydrate rich foods that you are eating, although in smaller quantities. Also, pack plenty of healthy snacks to munch on the trails, as children tend to get a little peckish when walking.

You are also going to need to make the hike a little more entertaining when trekking with children. Try to set up games such as I spy, moving hide and seek, 20 questions, or a miniature scavenger hunt that you can play as you go. You may also give them a task or job to complete. Counting birds, spotting interesting rock formations, or pointing out water sources can be really engaging activities for the young ones. Make it a little competitive by naming a winner at the end of the trail. You are also going to need to stop more frequently with a child, as they will generally not be able to keep pace with you for long periods. Try to keep the breaks brief, but have them more frequently to ensure you do not lose momentum. If you are hiking with one child, think about allowing them to bring a friend. This is a great way to keep them engaged and will add to the enjoyment they feel. This is a big responsibility, however, and you should ensure that you alert the friend's parents to the fact that you will be hiking and let them know where and when you will be going. Prioritize fun on these hikes, as you do not want to discourage your children going forward.

Pets

We hike with our dog all the time and he absolutely loves it. It adds such a wonderful dynamic for us, and if you do have a dog, then they may make a wonderful hiking companion. The most important factor in taking your pet on a hike is ensuring that the trail is in fact pet friendly. Beyond that, there are some other significant considerations. Unless your dog is very obedient and well trained, always keep them on a leash. On crowded trails, keep the leash short and ensure your dog is close to you at all times. When the trail is a bit more isolated, you may consider letting out the leash a little so that they can explore a bit more. If your dog is not well socialized with people or other dogs, you should be sure to keep them under close control.

Don't forget the poop bags and make sure to clean up after your pets. There is nothing worse than stepping in a dog dropping in the wake of a careless dog owner. You should also take water for your pet and ensure that they are drinking regularly. Dogs' noses and gums will become dry when dehydrated, and this is a clear sign that it is time to stop and break out the bowl. If your dog is panting severely and having trouble breathing, then they may have heat exhaustion. In this case, you should quickly move them to a shady area and pour small amounts of cool water over their bodies. Allow them to drink at intervals and ensure their body temperature is lowering. Preparing them for a hike is a great way to prevent any such ailments. Take them for increasingly longer walks leading up to the hike and consider getting a vet's perspective on their ability to take on a trail.

When in the country with your dog, it is likely that you will come across other animals, both domestic and wild. This can be very dangerous for your dog and so you should have them on a leash at all times if this is a possibility. If you spot any animals up ahead, grip the leash tight and stop walking. Do not approach animals with your dog and allow them to move off at a safe distance. If they are stationary, try to beat a wide circle around them and avoid confrontations at all costs. It is also important that your dog's health is protected when out and about. Your dog needs to be fully vaccinated. Research the requirements in your local area, but around the world, parvovirus, lyme disease, distemper, rabies, and leptospirosis are common because these are diseases caught from wild animals and insects. Ensure, too, that you carefully check your dog, and yourself, for ticks upon completion. Ticks can be really nasty and lyme disease is no joke. If either you or your dog are bitten by a tick, be sure to seek medical attention as soon as possible. We have had some very close calls with ticks! You should also remove any burs or grass seeds from your pet's hair, as these can get matted easily into their fur and can be awfully hard to remove the longer they are present. Also consider joint medication and paw care. If your dog's paws become dry and cracked, be sure to moisturize them to ensure they can walk comfortably. Lastly, never allow your dogs to eat any plants or drink from water sources on the trail. Besides poisonous plants there is a real risk of water-borne bacteria on hiking trails and you do not want to hike with a sick pooch!

Chapter 10:

Overnight Hiking

Once you are a confident day hiker, you may look to the next big challenge: spending nights out on the trails. The stakes will be higher but the reward will be too! Overnight hiking has a number of very important considerations, and forgetting something important is going to have deeper consequences. If you are thinking about branching out, then we suggest that you first talk to someone with experience. Perhaps go to your local outdoor shop and discuss your chosen trail with them. You may also look to online forums or social media groups for advice. When overnight hiking, we will never recommend solo hiking. Even veterans need a companion when hitting the trails for several days at a time. If you cannot think of companions to invite, consider signing up to a group with a guide. Let's take a look at the most important considerations.

Key Considerations

Firstly, you are going to need to sleep somewhere. Some hiking trails may have hostels along the way. Others may require you to take a tent. Perhaps for your first few overnight hikes you should try the hostel route. This will allow you to carry less in your pack and leave behind all sleeping gear, in addition to most cooking gear. When selecting hostels for a hike, you may want to look at trails that have this in mind already. You will find many hikes online and in forums that snake their ways from hostel to hostel. This is going to make the booking process a lot simpler and you will be able to be more sure that the trail is walkable. If you are going to book hostels yourself and make your way between them on trails of your choosing, we highly recommend getting a topographical map of the entire area and studying it carefully until you are satisfied that you know the way and will be able to reach each hostel in a day's walk.

Next, you will need a sleeping bag or an alternative. Sleeping bags are your best bet for staying warm, although they can be very bulky to carry and take up a lot of space. If you are hiking in warm weather, you may not want to take a sleeping bag, as you may risk overheating in the night. There are some great lightweight alternatives. A camping quilt for one, is like a blanket, although it is designed to retain warmth a little better. These are far easier to carry and a little more adaptable to both cold and hot climates. You may also simply bring a blanket from home, though you should make sure that this will keep you warm enough as you trek. If you like the idea of being encased when you sleep, you may consider a sleeping bag liner that you cover with a blanket or quilt. These are really lightweight and easy to carry and you can cover yourself easily. Another option is a bivy bag. These can also replace your sleeping bag and allow you to completely cover yourself in a weather-proof bag. In hotter weather, this should keep you sufficiently warm, however, in colder climates, you will definitely need a quilt or blanket too. These are fairly bulky, too, however, you will save space by just taking this instead of a tent and sleeping bag.

You also need to consider sleeping mats. Many people buy the cheapest yoga mat they can find and take these on their adventures. We would recommend digging a little deeper, as camping-specific mats are often designed with ridges or bumps for comfort and retaining warmth. Your two main options are permanent mats and inflatables. Better quality permanent mats are going to be harder to carry and less comfortable but they eliminate any risk. Inflatables are going to require a little effort at the end of the day and will be very easy to carry. However, if you are hiking over rough terrain, you will be at risk of a puncture that will mean you have to sleep on the hard ground with very little protection. Consider these options carefully and weigh up these pros and cons.

When camping, you will need to think about food too. Again, take only non-perishables and prioritize lean proteins and carbohydrates. Spaghetti and other pasta are lightweight and easily carried. If you are going to take meats, try to either take cured meats in airtight packaging or tinned meats such as tuna or mackerel. Bear in mind that once these are out of the tin, they are no longer non-perishable. For vegans and vegetarians, beans, chickpeas, and other legumes are a great tinned food that will give you ample protein. Take lots of snack foods such as trail mix, nuts, and granola bars. Try to eat constantly during the day and prepare one meal after the day is done.

On overnight hikes you have to take cooking equipment as well. If you are going to be able to make a fire safely, then you will need to take only a lightweight pot to cook in. Mountain trails are often sparse in terms of firewood, and in this case, you may need to take a lightweight gas cooker. These are really effective, but make sure that you take enough gas and a reserve canister as well. Many hikers like to take small kettles or a moka pot for tea and coffee. If you love a hot beverage, then consider these, but otherwise leave them behind to save on pack space. Everything is going to be a trade-off. If you take something, you will have to carry it the entire time, so think carefully about what you actually need. We have completed overnight hikes where we returned home only to unpack several items that we did not use at all.

Water is always going to be a big consideration. If you are on a lengthy multiday hike, it may not always be possible to carry enough water the entire time, and so you need to think about your options. Water sources you find on a hike may not always be sanitary. Chlorine tablets or boiling water can be a great way to ensure you are drinking clean water. Collecting water in the evenings and boiling it on the fire is the best way to ensure you are hydrating yourself safely. You may consider a filter too. Reverse osmosis filters are the best, as these will remove bacteria and viruses from water. These filters can even remove salt if you are getting desperate. Simpler filters can be effective on high altitude hikes where you are drinking mountain water, but always be careful with these. Finally, there are UV light treatment options that allow you to purify water. These, too, are only recommended for clear mountain water, as the cloudier the water, the more likely bacteria is protected from the light.

Something that is not often considered but is absolutely vital is a sleeping system. Now, this is not about setting an alarm clock overnight, but rather structuring how you sleep when the time comes. You want to consider this carefully and maximize the space available to you as well as comfort. A bad night's sleep on the trail is going to start you off on the wrong foot the next day and should be avoided at all costs. When devising a sleeping system, you need to prioritize comfort, moisture resistance, warmth, compressibility, and ease of deploying and packing. Take a test run at home with all your gear and identify what is superfluous and leave it behind. On overnight trails, you do not want to carry anything that is unnecessary.

Hygiene is another really important aspect of overnight hiking and can be a little challenging in places. Before you go to bed each night, make sure to change your clothes. Going to bed dirty is a recipe for nasty sleeping gear that will get worse as you progress. You also need to take more specialized hygiene products to ensure you do not sully the water sources on the route. Be sure to take biodegradable detergents for any laundry you may be doing and get specialized hiking shampoo and soap. You will probably need to use a river for the purposes of washing or simply rinsing yourself with a collection of water. You need to be wary of the water you are using, as it may well be a source of drinking water. Take some water to a different location and rinse off with a small tub. You should also take plastic bags that allow you to keep your dirty clothes separate so as not to dirty your fresh gear.

Women have a little more to consider when spending nights on the trail. Never forget hygiene products such as tampons or pads, even if you are sure you won't be on your cycle during the hike. Women are also more susceptible to yeast infections and so you might consider taking more changes of underwear than necessary. Women also have a slightly more intricate operation ahead of them when relieving themselves. If you would like to be able to urinate without exposing half of your body, you might consider a pee funnel or equivalent which will allow you to urinate without the exposure. A quick-dry microfiber towel is going to be a huge asset for washing daily, but also a miniature one can be used as a reusable toilet paper alternative.

The last thing to consider is motivation and inspiration. By the third day of a hike, you might feel your enthusiasm waning and it is important to be able to keep in good spirits. We are both avid readers and some of our favorite books about adventure and the natural world help to inspire us to persevere through lengthier hikes. You may also want to customize your itinerary to suit your interests. Setting stops at lakes, waterfalls, or beautiful scenery is a great way to start the day off the right way. You may also look for ways to include hobbies on the trail. Simple things like watercolor painting, knitting, or even fishing can all be done along a hike and will improve your mood and thus motivation as you march along. Our last piece of advice is to look inward. Remind yourself why you have chosen this challenge and the reward you will feel once completed. Longer hikes are some of the most incredible experiences and you should remind yourself of that often.

Conclusion

Now that you know the basics, it's time to set out. We hope that if you have taken anything away from this book, it's a sense of confidence in your ability to do these things. You can complete an all-day hike and we hope you believe this too. You have learned all about the preparation required, from the physical elements to packing your gear. You know what to wear and what not to, as well as how to choose and plan the perfect hike for yourself. You will be able to keep yourself safe as a solo hiker, too, and you know all about how to handle emergency situations adequately. You know about the weather and how to avoid disasters in rain and snow, as well as how to dress to protect yourself against the elements. You know all about the food you should take on a hike and how to make sure you are adequately hydrated.

You also know how to navigate effectively and prevent the risk of getting lost on the trail. You know how to tell where you can and cannot go while on a hike and how to deal with animal encounters. You know all the etiquette you need, and you understand that you need to help to sustain the natural world around you so that many more people can derive the same joy that you have. You know the consequences for non-compliance but also know that you should protect the world irrespective of these. You are ready to take on the trails with your children, too, or with your trusty pooch. With a little practice, you will be ready for an overnight hiking adventure too! We really hope that you have learned some important lessons from this book and that you use them to develop a love for hiking the way we have. It really is a wonderful hobby, and the more you get out there, the more enjoyment you will get. Now, grab the packing list and head out there!

Bonuses

Training Schedule

Monday	Tuesday	Wednesday	Thursday	Friday
E.g. Cardio Day: 15 min run, 5 min skipping, 3 sets of 10 burpees, 3 sets 10 squats	*E.g. Strength Training:* 4 sets of 10 pushups, 2 sets of 10 pullups, 1 minute plank pose, 3 sets of 10 crunches	*etc.*		

Monday	Tuesday	Wednesday	Thursday	Friday

First Trip Checklist

Essentials:
- First Aid Kit
- Sun Protection (Sunscreen and Hat)
- Navigation (Map/GPS/Compass)
- Water
- Food
- Flashlight/Headlamp
- Waterproof Jacket/Umbrella
- Fully Charged Mobile Phone
- Lighter/Matches
- Identification Card/Document
- Permits (if required)
- Trowel and Toilet Paper (for longer hikes)
- Bag for Waste
- Itinerary

Potential Extras:
- Multitool/knife
- Emergency Shelter (for longer day hikes)
- Space Blanket
- Lip Balm

- Personal Medication
- Walking Poles

Hiking with Children:
- Extra Snacks and Water
- Warm Clothing for Your Children
- Games

Hiking With Pets:
- Lead
- Water Bowl
- Treats
- Muzzle (if required)

First Aid Cheat Sheet

Checklist:

- Bandages/Gauze/Band-Aids
- Disinfectant
- Hand Sanitizer
- Pain Killers
- Anti-Inflammatories
- Antihistamines
- Fungal Cream/Ointment
- Bug Spray
- Sting Ointment
- Tweezers/Scissors/Safety Pins
- Aftersun
- Epipen or Specific Medication (as required)
- List of Emergency Contacts
- Split/Pressure Socks

Cheat Sheet:

- Remain calm
- Establish severity of the injury
- Are you able to treat the injury?
- Are you able to continue?

- Do you need to call for help?
- Has anyone been bitten or stung by an insect or animal?
- Do you need to spend the night?
- Find a sheltered spot to wait
- Reevaluate once injury is treated
- Devise a plan
- Find the quickest route home

References

Allred, B. (2022, March 23). *What snakes live in Europe and which is the largest?* AZ Animals. https://a-z-animals.com/blog/what-snakes-live-in-europe-and-which-is-the-largest/

Backpacker Editors. (2015, January 27). *How to get in shape for hiking | Train for hiking and backpacking.* Backpacker. https://www.backpacker.com/skills/backpacking-fitness/how-to-get-in-shape-for-hiking/

Backroads. (n.d.). *Top hiking stretches - stretching exercises | Backroads.* Www.backroads.com. https://www.backroads.com/pro-tips/hiking/top-hiking-stretches

Basu Mallick, C. (2022, June 3). *What is GPS (global positioning system)? Meaning, Types, Working, Examples, and Applications.* Spiceworks. https://www.spiceworks.com/tech/iot/articles/what-is-gps/

Bor, K. (2020, April 1). *Hiking alone: solo hiking benefits and safety tips.* Bearfoot Theory. https://bearfoottheory.com/hiking-alone/

Boseley, S. (2019, January 14). *Nutritionists launch portion size guide to tackle overeating.* The Guardian; The Guardian. https://www.theguardian.com/science/2019/jan/14/nutritionists-launch-portion-size-guide-to-tackle-overeating

Boulware, D. R. (2004). Gender differences among long distance backpackers: A prospective study of women Appalachian Trail backpackers. *Wilderness & Environmental Medicine, 15*(3), 175–180. https://www.ncbi.nlm.nih.gov/pmc/articles/PMC1946964/

Brunton Compass Clinic. (n.d.). *101: Types of compasses.* Brunton. https://www.brunton.com/blogs/blog/brunton-basic-compass-clinic-types-of-compasses

Bumgardner, W. (2018, December 18). *5 Things you should not drink when walking.* Verywell Fit. https://www.verywellfit.com/six-things-you-should-not-drink-when-walking-3435429

Bumgardner, W. (2020, August 3). *The health benefits and risks of downhill walking.* Verywell Fit. https://www.verywellfit.com/how-to-walk-downhill-3435572#:~:text=When%20you%20walk%20uphill%2C%20you

Camotrek Staff. (2021, June 26). *How to choose the best hiking backpack for your adventures? (in 2021).* Camotrek | Hiking and Tactical Gear Guides, Reviews & Skills. https://camotrek.com/blogs/news/how-to-choose-the-best-hiking-backpack/

CDC. (2019, June 24). *Lightning safety.* Centers for Disease Control and Prevention. https://www.cdc.gov/nceh/features/lightning-safety/index.html

CDC. (2021, December 17). *Water treatment options when hiking, camping or traveling | Drinking Water | Healthy Water | CDC.* Www.cdc.gov. https://www.cdc.gov/healthywater/drinking/travel/index.html#:~:text=Boiling%20Water

CDC. (2022, April 27). *Benefits of physical activity.* Centers for Disease Control and Prevention. https://www.cdc.gov/physicalactivity/basics/pa-health/index.htm#:~:text=Being%20physically%20active%20can%20improve

Corliss, J. (2018, November 13). *Health benefits of hiking: raise your heart rate and your mood - Harvard Health Blog.* Harvard Health Blog.

https://www.health.harvard.edu/blog/health-benefits-of-hiking-raise-your-heart-rate-and-your-mood-2016092810414

Cummings, M. (n.d.). *Take your kids hiking: 10 tips to make the adventure fun for the whole family | The Wilderness Society*. Www.wilderness.org. Retrieved October 12, 2022, from https://www.wilderness.org/articles/article/take-your-kids-hiking-10-tips-make-adventure-fun-whole-family

Curtis, R. (1998). Guide to general emergency procedures. In *The Backpacker's Field Manual A Comprehensive Guide to Mastering Backcountry Skills*. Random House. https://www.princeton.edu/~oa/safety/emergency.shtml

Decathlon Staff. (n.d.). *Keep dry when out hiking: check out our 8 tips*. Www.quechua.com. Retrieved October 11, 2022, from https://www.quechua.com/keep-dry-when-out-hiking-check-out-our-8-tips

Decide Outside. (n.d.). 8 Sleeping bag alternatives: Ultralight, Regular, DIY | Decide Outside. *Decide Outside*. Retrieved October 24, 2022, from https://decideoutside.com/ultralight-sleeping-bag-alternatives/#:~:text=The%20most%20viable%20alternative%20to

Elms-Smith, C. (2022, May 25). *9 Tips for hiking in bad weather*. Tracks Less Travelled. https://trackslesstravelled.com/hiking-in-bad-weather/

EMS. (n.d.). *Understanding weather when hiking | Eastern Mountain Sports*. Www.ems.com. Retrieved October 19, 2022, from https://www.ems.com/understanding-weather-when-hiking

Feeney, J. (2016, November 26). *Knowing your limits in the outdoors*. The Hiking Society. https://www.thehikingsociety.com.au/2016/11/26/knowing-limits-outdoors/

Gibeault, S. (2019, September 29). *Hiking with your dog: tips for hitting the trail in a safe and fun way.* American Kennel Club. https://www.akc.org/expert-advice/lifestyle/tips-for-hiking-with-your-dog/

Gifford, E. (2022, February 11). *Hiking gear for kids: what outdoor gear do kids really need?* Go Hike Virginia. https://gohikevirginia.com/hiking-gear-kids/

Guest Authors. (n.d.). *What to do if you get lost hiking | GORE-TEX Brand.* Www.gore-Tex.com. https://www.gore-tex.com/blog/what-to-do-if-you-get-lost-hiking

Guest Authors. (2017). *How to build the best hiking first aid kit.* Gore-Tex.com; GORE-TEX. https://www.gore-tex.com/blog/hiking-first-aid-kit

Guru, R., Kumar, A., & Kumar, R. (2021). Functional textile for active wear clothing. In *www.intechopen.com*. IntechOpen. https://www.intechopen.com/chapters/75976

Handley, C. (2019). *Pros and cons of hiking with trekking poles.* CleverHiker. https://www.cleverhiker.com/blog/pros-and-cons-of-hiking-with-trekking-poles#:~:text=Poles%20can%20help%20you%20keep

Hepworth, A. (2022, April 6). *What to wear hiking, for all seasons, weather forecasts & destinations.* PureWow. https://www.purewow.com/fashion/what-to-wear-hiking

Hillwalk Tours. (2019, April 14). *Common hiking injuries 2019 update - a Hillwalk Guide from Hillwalk Tours.* Walking Hiking Blog. https://www.hillwalktours.com/walking-hiking-blog/common-hiking-injuries/

Hilsman, A. (2021, March 29). *Feminine hygiene while backpacking.* Green Mountain Club.

https://www.greenmountainclub.org/feminine-hygiene-backcountry-womens-backpacking/#:~:text=Sanitation%3A%20Women%20are%20more%20prone

Holt, S. (2020, April 14). *7 Exercises to get in shape for hiking.* Appalachian Mountain Club. https://www.outdoors.org/resources/amc-outdoors/health-and-safety/home-workout-for-hiking/

Honan, C. (n.d.). *Hiking techniques.* The Hiking Life. https://www.thehikinglife.com/hiking-and-backpacking-skills/hiking-techniques/

Hostel walking: what it is, organising a trip and kit list. (2019, June 17). Countryfile.com. https://www.countryfile.com/go-outdoors/hostel-walking/

How to find your coordinates on your cell phone. (2022, July 14). Emelee Outdoors. https://emeleeoutdoors.com/blogs/news/how-to-find-your-coordinates-on-your-cell-phone-or-common-apps-and-send-to-someone

How to Start a campfire without matches or a lighter. (2018, September 19). Scout Life Magazine. https://scoutlife.org/video-audio/15418/how-to-start-a-fire-without-matches/#:~:text=Start%20with%20a%20big%2C%20loose

Inspiration Outdoors. (2014, February 17). *Water bottles vs bladders.* Inspiration Outdoors. https://www.inspirationoutdoors.com.au/blog/water-bottles-vs-bladders/#:~:text=Water%20bottles%20are%20less%20likely

Jackson, J. (2019, October 9). *How much water to take on a hike? | Hiking NZ.* Hikingnewzealand.com. https://hikingnewzealand.com/blog/how-much-water-to-take-on-a-hike/

Jacobs, M. (n.d.). *Baby proof South Africa*. Baby Proof. Retrieved October 18, 2022, from https://www.babyproof.co.za/common-poisonous-plants-in-south-africa/

Kruchten, L. (2016, August 1). *The best and worst foods to fuel you before a hike*. Spoon University. https://spoonuniversity.com/lifestyle/the-best-and-worst-foods-to-fuel-you-before-a-hike

Lee, H. (n.d.). *8 Tips for preventing athlete's foot*. Www.bellevuefootdoctor.com. Retrieved October 18, 2022, from https://www.bellevuefootdoctor.com/blog/8-tips-for-preventing-athletes-foot

MAYO Clinic. (n.d.). *Athlete's foot - diagnosis and treatment*. Www.mayoclinic.org. Retrieved October 18, 2022, from https://www.mayoclinic.org/diseases-conditions/athletes-foot/diagnosis-treatment/drc-20353847#:~:text=Wash%20your%20feet%20twice%20a

McGivney, A. (2011, August 25). *How to walk*. Backpacker. https://www.backpacker.com/skills/how-to-walk/

McMillan, N. (2020, May 12). *How to optimize your break time while hiking*. FarOut. https://faroutguides.com/break-time-optimization/#:~:text=My%20Big%20Mile%20Hiking%20Plan&text=Try%20to%20keep%20breaks%20close

Mountain Club of South Africa. (n.d.). *Description of grades*. Mountain Club of South Africa - South Cape. Retrieved October 17, 2022, from https://southcape.mcsa.org.za/description-of-grades/

Moye, J. (2019, April 11). *Why some lost hikers live and others die*. Adventure. https://www.nationalgeographic.com/adventure/article/hikers-survival-tips

National Park Service. (2019, May 29). *Benefits of hiking - trails & hiking (U.S. National Park Service)*. Www.nps.gov. https://www.nps.gov/subjects/trails/benefits-of-hiking.htm#:~:text=Being%20in%20nature%20can%20boost

National Weather Service: National Oceanic and Atmospheric Administration. (n.d.). *Understanding lightning: Thunder*. Www.weather.gov. https://www.weather.gov/safety/lightning-science-thunder#:~:text=If%20you%20count%20the%20number

NCSL. (2014). *States with littering penalties*. Ncsl.org. https://www.ncsl.org/research/environment-and-natural-resources/states-with-littering-penalties.aspx

Newgent, J. (2019). *5 Food tips for camping and hiking*. Eatright.org. https://www.eatright.org/food/planning-and-prep/snack-and-meal-ideas/food-tips-for-camping-and-hiking

NI Direct Government Services. (2015, November 10). *The countryside code nidirect*. Www.nidirect.gov.uk. https://www.nidirect.gov.uk/articles/countryside-code

NPS. (n.d.). *Hiking etiquette (U.S. National Park Service)*. Www.nps.gov. https://www.nps.gov/articles/hikingetiquette.htm

NZ Health Ministry. (n.d.). *Stinging nettles*. Ministry of Health NZ. https://www.health.govt.nz/your-health/conditions-and-treatments/accidents-and-injuries/bites-and-stings/stinging-nettles

Parks and Recreation San Diego County. (2017). *Before & after a hike*. Sdparks.org. https://www.sdparks.org/content/sdparks/en/news-events/news-stories/BeforeandAfteraHike.html

Petruzzello, M. (n.d.). *7 Dangerous plants you should never touch*. Encyclopedia Britannica. https://www.britannica.com/list/7-plants-you-cant-even-touch

REI Co-op. (n.d.). *How to prevent and care for blisters | REI Co-op*. REI. Retrieved October 18, 2022, from https://www.rei.com/learn/expert-advice/blister-prevention-care.html#:~:text=Dress%20the%20blister%20like%20you

REI Staff. (2017, October 17). *How to go to the bathroom in the woods*. Rei.com; REI. https://www.rei.com/learn/expert-advice/hygiene-sanitation.html

REI Staff. (2019a, July 8). *How to use a compass: compass/map navigation*. REI; REI. https://www.rei.com/learn/expert-advice/navigation-basics.html

REI Staff. (2019b, September 9). *Hiking boots: how to choose hiking shoes*. REI; REI. https://www.rei.com/learn/expert-advice/hiking-boots.html

Renwick, W. (2022, October 3). *Best waterproof jackets for 2022*. Outdoors Magic. https://outdoorsmagic.com/article/best-waterproof-jackets/

Safety when walking with young children – walking & hiking Information. (n.d.). Walking and Hiking Information. Retrieved October 23, 2022, from https://www.whi.org.uk/safe-walking/safety-when-walking-with-young-children/#:~:text=Make%20sure%20that%20you%20take

Seattle Children's Hospital. (2022, March 17). *Bruises and cuts*. Seattle Children's Hospital. https://www.seattlechildrens.org/conditions/a-z/bruises-and-cuts/

Snakebite Institute. (2017). *Snakebite - African Snakebite Institute.* African Snakebite Institute. https://www.africansnakebiteinstitute.com/snakebite/

Spicer, D. (n.d.). *Best backpacking sleep system: how to put together a good one.* Hiking for Her. Retrieved October 24, 2022, from https://www.hiking-for-her.com/backpacking-sleep-system.html

Stevenson, J. (2018, August 8). *A backpacker's guide to personal hygiene while camping.* Backpacker. https://www.backpacker.com/skills/prof-hike-a-backpacker-s-guide-to-smart-personal-hygiene/

Stuehler, S. (2020, July 1). *Trail permits: what you need to know.* FarOut. https://faroutguides.com/trail-permits/

Stump, M. (n.d.). *How to choose hiking socks.* REI. https://www.rei.com/learn/expert-advice/backpacking-socks.html

Tahoe Trail Bar. (2022, July 11). *Should you drink coffee before a hike?* Tahoe Trail Bar. https://tahoetrailbar.com/blogs/news/should-you-drink-coffee-before-a-hike#:~:text=Having%20a%20cup%20of%20coffee

Top Ten Selects. (2020, August 20). *10 Best weather apps in 2022: tried and tested.* Www.top10.com. https://www.top10.com/weather-apps

VanDoren, C. (2022, February 21). *7 Healthy benefits of hiking you need to know.* The Manual. https://www.themanual.com/fitness/benefits-of-hiking/

Washington Trails Association. (n.d.-a). *Hiking 101: planning your hike.* Washington Trails Association. Retrieved October 12, 2022, from https://www.wta.org/go-outside/new-to-hiking/hiking-101-1/hiking-101-part-1-choosing-the-right-hike

Washington Trails Association. (n.d.-b). *Hiking maps and why you need them*. Washington Trails Association. https://www.wta.org/go-outside/trail-smarts/map-resource-page-hiking-maps-and-why-you-need-them

What to do in an emergency when hiking | Trespass advice. (n.d.). Www.trespass.com. https://www.trespass.com/advice/what-to-do-in-an-outdoors-emergency/

When to travel Worldwide. (2021, August 22). *Best time to hike [perfect weather, season, daytime, clothing]*. Any Travel Tips. https://www.anytraveltips.com/travel-listing/hike-best-time

Printed in Great Britain
by Amazon